D1086878

EASTER 1997

JESUIT
Family Album

Sketches of Chivalry
from the Early Society

By
Joseph F. MacDonnell, S.J.
Professor of Mathematics
Fairfield University

Printed and bound in the United States of America

Published by   CLAVIUS GROUP

Distributed by   Joseph F. MacDonnell, S.J.
                      Fairfield University
                      Fairfield, CT 06430

Library of Congress Cataloging-in-Publication Data

    MacDonnell, Joseph
    JESUIT FAMILY ALBUM
    Sketches of Chivalry from the Early Society
    by Joseph F. MacDonnell, S.J
    Includes bibliographical references.
    235 illustrations

Library of Congress Catalog Card Number: 97-66543

BX3706.2.m23

    1. Jesuits-History-16th-century
    2. Jesuits-History-17th-century
    3. Jesuits-History-18th-century

ISBN   0-9657731-0-8   paperback

Frontispiece from the 1679 book VESTIGIA MATHEMATICA by the Jesuit mathematician Jean König taken from the *Jesuitica Collection* at Loyola University Chicago. Around the circumference are etched the words: "**St. Ignatius Loyola, Author, Founder and first Superior General of the Society of Jesus, serving from 1540 to 31, July 1556.**" Under it is the famous *SUSCIPE* prayer of Ignatius.

Take, O Lord, and receive all my liberty,
my memory, my understanding, and my entire will.
Whatever I have or hold, You have given me; I restore it all to You
and surrender it wholly to be governed by Your will.
Give me only Your love and Your grace;
I am rich enough to ask for nothing more.

These sketches concerning 202 scientists, scholars, mathematicians, explorers, artists and martyrs of the early Society are dedicated to

The Clavius Group

whose devotion to research and teaching perpetuate a long Jesuit tradition of collaboration which was urged by the past General Congregation.

"We are grateful for this collaboration and are enriched by it. Jesuits are *men **for** others* and *men **with** others*."
(From the 1995 Jesuit General Congregation 34 held in Rome)

Table of Contents

102	Lecchi, Jean (1702-1776)	Italian mathematician
103	Ledesma, James (1519-1575)	Spanish theologian
104	LeMoyne, Simon (1604-1697)	French explorer
106	Lessius, Leonard (1554-1623)	Belgian theologian
107	Lewis, David (1617-1679)	English martyr
108	Linyères, Claude (1658-1746)	French counselor
108	Loyola, St. Ignatius (1490-1556)	Basque Founder
110	Lugo, John de (1583-1660)	Spanish scholar
111	Malagrida, Gabriel (1689-1761)	Italian confessor
112	Maldonado, John de (1534-1583)	Spanish theologian
113	Mancinelli, Ven. Jules (1558-1618)	Italian preacher
114	Mariana, John (1537-1624)	Spanish theologian
115	Marquette, Jacques (1637-1675)	French explorer
116	Mastrilli, Marcel (1603-1637)	Italian martyr
117	Maunoir, Bl. Julien (1606-1683)	French preacher
118	Mendez de Loyola, Balthasar (1531-1567)	Turkish confessor
119	Ménestrier, Claude (1631-1705)	French scholar
120	Mercurian, Everard (1514-1580)	Belgian Sup. General
121	Mesquita, S.G. James de (1553-1614)	Portuguese missions
121	Messari, John Baptist (1673-1723)	German martyr
122	Miki, St. Paul (1564-1597)	Japanese martyr
123	Molina, John (1740-1829)	Chilean scientist
124	Molina, Luis de (1535-1600)	Spanish theologian
125	Morse, Henry (1595-1645)	English martyr
126	Mulcaille, Philip (1727-1801)	Irish educator
127	Nadal, Jerome (1507-1580)	Spanish First Ten
129	Neale, Leonard (1747-1817)	American educator
130	Neumayr, Francis (1697-1765)	German dramatist
131	Nidhard, John (1607-1681)	Austrian counselor
131	Nieremberg, Eusebio (1595-1658)	Spanish theologian
132	Nobili, St. Robert de (1577-1656)	Italian missionary
133	Nobrega, Emmanuel (1517-1570)	Portuguese explorer
134	Noyelle, Charles de (1615-1686)	Belgian Sup. General
135	Ogilvie, St. John (1579-1615)	Scottish martyr
136	Oldcorne, Bl. Edward (1561-1606)	English martyr
137	Oliva, John Paul (1600-1681)	Italian Sup. General
138	Owen, St. Nicholas (?-1606)	English martyr
140	Pacheco, Bl. Francis (1565-1626)	Portuguese missions
141	Páez, Peter (1564-1622)	Spanish explorer
142	Page, Bl. Francis (?-1602)	Belgian martyr
143	Pallavicino, Sforza (1607-1667)	Italian historian
144	Parrenin, Dominic (1665-1741)	French missionary
145	Pázmány, Peter (1570-1637)	Hungarian educator
147	Persons, Robert (1546-1610)	English missionary
148	Petau, Dennis (1583-1652)	French scholar
149	Pickel, Ignatius (1736-1818)	German scientist
149	Pignatelli, St. Joseph (1737-1811)	Italian confessor
151	Pongrácz, St. Stephen (1583-1619)	Transylvanian mart.
152	Porée, Charles (1675-1741)	French poet
153	Possevino, Antonio (1533-1611)	Italian diplomat
156	Pozzo, Andrea (1640-1709)	Italian artist
158	Rapin, René (1621-1687)	French poet
159	Realino, St. Bernadine (1530-1616)	Italian educator
160	Regis, St. John Francis (1597-1640)	French preacher

Introduction

Even within Catholicism religious orders have been controversial since the founding of eremitical and monastic institutions some seventeen hundred years ago. No order has had more dedicated partisans or ardent enemies, however, than the Society of Jesus. Simply by being born in the sixteenth century, a century of intense religious conflict and bloodshed, the Society was bound to earn obloquy as well as praise and emulation.

One reason for both the suspicion and admiration in which the Society was held was its systemic cultivation of learning and the arts in the service of God. Other religious orders of course made significant contributions in these areas, but because the Society undertook formal schooling as a major ministry, the first order in the church to do so, it had - I use the word again - a systemic relationship to secular culture that no other order had. It also had a spirituality that sought "to find God in all things," as the Jesuits' founder Ignatius of Loyola expressed it, and thus was inclined to a course that to some seemed all too worldly.

In any case, these factors, plus many others, produced a remarkable array of individuals outstanding in many areas of human endeavor. Father MacDonnell has assembled *sketches* of over 200 of them, describing their achievements in a straightforward and positive way. The result is a enlightening panorama, a window into a corporate culture that few people in the late twentieth century have any idea ever existed.

John W. O'Malley, S.J.
Weston School of Theology
Cambridge, Massachusetts

"One might well argue that the *Society of Jesus,* rather than the *Accademia del Cimento* or the *Royal Society*, was the first true scientific society . . . in [its] ability to collect observations and objects from a worldwide network of informants. . . . If scientific collaboration was one of the outgrowths of the scientific revolution, the Jesuits deserve a large share of the credit.

(*God and Nature* by David Lindberg, 1986 p.155)

The Society of Jesus in the 17th century contained within its ranks an astonishing number of enthusiastic students of the natural world. Indeed, for the first 60 years of the century, the Jesuits were the only scientific society in existence anywhere. At a time when experimental science was decidedly unfashionable, Jesuits were charting sunspots, calibrating pendulums, timing the fall of weights off towers, and devising a variety of ingenious inventions. Indeed, in the fields of geometry, optics, magnetism, cartography, mechanics, and earth sciences, most of the principal authorities throughout the century were members of the Society of Jesus. The Jesuits were a remarkably bold and imaginative scientific body.

(*Jesuit science in the age of Galileo* by William Ashworth, 1986 p.5)

Preface

As is evident from this collection of sketches, Jesuits come in a great variety of shapes, sizes and dispositions. Some were made bishops (over the protests of the Jesuit Curia) and cardinals, one even became a cardinal and then a king (King Jan III Kasimierz of Poland). Besides some were declared by the Church to be (with symbols used in brackets)

Saints	**(St.)**
Blesseds	**(Bl.)**
Venerables	**(Ven.)**
Servants of God	**(S.G.)**

In these sketches it is worth noticing the many Coadjutor Brothers who have enriched the Society greatly for 450 years by their skills as administrators, chemists, botanists, cooks, porters, sacristans, artists, astronomers, librarians and, above all, models of religious dedication who have inspired their fellow Priest-Jesuits.

Many remarkable Jesuits are omitted here because no pictures are available but they are celebrated in other ways. From 40 countries more than 600 commemorative stamps, 35 lunar craters, 2 Paris metro stations and 2 statues in Statuary Hall in Washington, D.C., innumerable statues, and city streets have been named to honor Jesuits. This book presents the variety of ways these 202 vibrant (mostly young) men from different backgrounds showed their dedication to the Society of Jesus and to the service of their neighbor. It is a record of their wit, courage, intelligence and persistence in spreading the Good News.

Various opinions concerning Jesuits

The English historian Robert Southy in his *History of Brazil* spoke of the Jesuits and their disastrous Suppression in 1773 with very un-British enthusiasm. What his comment lacked in ecumenism, it made up for in clarity.

". . . the sanctity of the (Jesuit) end proposed, and the heroism and perseverance with which it was pursued, deserve the highest admiration . . . It was the Jesuits' fate to be attacked with equal enmity by the unbelieving scoffers on one side, and by the all-believing bigots and blockheads of their own idolatrous Church on the other."

Jesuits had many interesting enemies. A good example is provided by one of their vacillating graduates, Voltaire. C.J. McNaspy in his *Lost Cities of Paraguay* quotes Voltaire's enthusiastic evaluation of Jesuits. "The establishment in Paraguay by the Spanish Jesuits appears alone, in some way, the triumph of humanity . . . and gave a new spectacle to the world." But a later Voltaire boasted of purging France of the Jesuits and hoped to release France from "that stupid power, the (Catholic) Church." As a matter of fact Voltaire was giving himself too much credit. The real cause for the Suppression of the Jesuits in 1773 lay more with the enemies of Jesuits within the Church. In 1773 the Church did not collapse and the Jesuits did eventually survive the Suppression. Like Montesquieu before him, Voltaire called upon a member of this same Jesuit Society he helped to suppress, to make sure that he "not be buried as an outcast in disgrace". Voltaire then signed a retraction so that he could be buried in a Catholic ceremony. More than once have Jesuits graciously buried those who prematurely thought they had buried the Society of Jesus.

The Philosophical Transactions of the Royal Society of London, whose glory it was "neither to deceive nor be deceived", took Jesuits very seriously. This is clear from the number of publications by and articles about Jesuits in the *Transactions* as well as the number of Jesuit books and articles translated into English for the use of the Royal Society. In fact, editor Oldenburg felt he had to apologize to his anti-Jesuit readers for printing the works of these fearsome men "whose goal it is to propagate their faith, enrich themselves with their craft. But, to recompense their destruction, Jesuits send useful intelligence from all parts of the world." A more genial sentiment was expressed by another Royal Society member, the physicist Robert Boyle: "The Jesuits have as prosperously addicted themselves to science as to divinity." Another version of Jesuits is presented by the Bollandists who wrote about the lives of saintly Jesuits. Surely the truth about Jesuits must lie somewhere in between (probably closer to the Bollandists viewpoint).

Sources of these sketches

Although the forerunner of camera theory came from the work of an early Jesuit, Athanasius Kircher's *camera obscura*, our familiar *box camera* did not appear until 1888 long after the Suppression of the Jesuits, so it was unusual to have pictures of anyone in the 16th, 17th and 18th centuries. This makes the large number of Jesuit portraits all the more impressive. These pictures are sometimes found in history books. Not all, but many of them came from Alfred Hamy's *Galerie Illustree*, a rare century-old work concerning famous Jesuits. This huge tome is part of the *Jesuitana* (Jesuit Collection) found in the *John J. Burns Library* of Boston College which was graciously made available to me by the Burns Library director Robert O'Neill. I had access to another edition from the Loyola University Chicago *Jesuitica* due to the kindness of Brother Michael Grace, S.J., director of the *Collection of Rare Books* at Loyola. Celebrating the 350th anniversary of the Order, the French Jesuit Alfred Hamy, S.J. described the lives of 400 well-known Jesuits in his 1875 *Essai sur l'Iconographie de la Companie de Jesus.* Later in 1893 he published a collection of their portraits in his *Galerie Illustree*. A 1675 book, *Societas Jesu,* about early Jesuits martyrs by Mathia Tanner, S.J. provided more pictures. Especially helpful for the stories were Carol Sommervogel's 14-volume *Bibliography* concerning Jesuit writings, Ludwig Koch's *Jesuiten Lexicon*, Joseph Tylenda's *Saints and Blessed of the Society* and William Bangert's *History of the Society* of Jesus. At the end of each entry the specific sources I used for writing the sketch are indicated by eleven triliteral abbreviations (**Ban, Bas, DSB, Ham, JLx, McR, JLP, O'M, Som, Tan, Tyl**) which are documented in my bibliography. Many of these SKETCHES can also be previewed on World Wide Web at the URL address: http://204.142.194.96/faculty/jmac/jp

I want especially to thank Joan Hanlon and fellow Jesuits Joseph Ryan, Vincent Burns, Donald Lynch and James Blaetler who patiently read my stories and offered many excellent suggestions. Their work would have to be characterized as nothing less than chivalrous.

José de Acosta
(Spanish: 1540-1600)

José de Acosta

José is called the *Pliny of the New World* because of his book *Natural and Moral History of the Indies* which provided the first detailed description of the geography and culture of Latin America, Aztec history and - of all things - the uses of coca. For his work on altitude sickness in the Andes he is listed as one of the pioneers of modern aeronautical medicine. José was far ahead of his time in the selection and description of his observations. Not satisfied, however, with mere descriptions, he tried to explain causes. José was one of the earliest geophysicists, having been among the first to observe, record and analyze earthquakes, volcanoes, tides, currents, magnetic declinations and meteorological phenomena. He denied the commonly held opinion that earthquakes and volcanoes originated from the same cause. José had an interesting explanation for the origin of the world's trade winds, and offered the earliest scientific explanation of the trade winds in the tropics. José traveled extensively through Peru, Bolivia, Chile and Mexico; he was the first European to systematize the geography of the New World.

Since José gave the first detailed description of the Mexican ideograms he can be legitimately called the first of the true Americanists. He learned enough of the indigenous cultures to write a trilingual catechism. Experts on American ethnology have praised José Acosta's insightful understanding of the origins of the Native Americans: that they came from Asia by way of a now-submerged land connection with Alaska, and the fact that they then switched from hunting to urban living and built the magnificent cities that the Spanish conquistadors found. A prominent ethnologist said: "It was an astonishing bit of scholarly deduction for the time, given the absence of knowledge about the existence of such a land bridge." (Ban, DSB, JLx, O'M, Som)

Francis   Alegre

Francis   Alegre
(Mexican: 1729-1788)

This brilliant scholar was forced to leave Mexico in 1767 when Spain exiled all Jesuits from its colonies. Francis along with Abad, Clavijero, Landivar, Maneiro, and other Jesuits banished from Mexico between 1767 to 1816 did not lead any revolts against their Spanish leaders, but from their places of exile, they produced literary works which convinced the world that their native land was very different from Spain and that Mexicans were entitled to their own way of life. The profound importance of these Jesuits in establishing an intellectual climate for Mexico's *Age of Independence* is a matter of history. Francis in many ways recapitulates the artistic and cultural possibilities latent within colonial Mexico. He is at once a dedicated classicist and historian and also a man who developed and maintained intellectual integrity by serious and original scholarship in many fields. His work and that of his Jesuit companions and their students reveal the richness of culture, and the universality of intellectual concerns that colonial Mexican society gave birth to in the last decades of Spanish domination.

Francis showed an abiding interest in the literatures of Europe and America in English, Italian, French, Portuguese and Spanish. His comparative method prefigures by half a century the theories of comparative literature to be later elaborated in France. His approach set a pattern for the study of world literature. Scholars after Francis Alegre, especially those of the 19th century, exerted a great effort to flesh out the comparative and historical investigations that Alegre suggested in his *Arte poetica*. For these reasons Alegre deserves credit as a significant literary critic not only within the framework of Mexican literary history but within literary history itself. A century after his death all his unpublished works were collected and published. His major contribution was a very valuable history of Mexico. Francis, one of New Spain's most accomplished scholars, at one time had a crater on the moon named in his honor. The crater is located in the sixth octant of the early editions of lunar maps, but has recently been renamed. (Ban, DSB, Ham, JLx, Som; also *Francisco Javier Alegre* by Allan Deck)

Apollinaris & companions

Ven. Apollinaris de Almeida
(Spanish: 1587-1638)

Apollinaris went to Ethiopia as bishop to succeed the Jesuit Patriarch Affonso Mendez during the reign of the Negus (Emperor) Susenyos who had become a Catholic. Because of Catholicism's strict moral code, most of the political leaders and wealthy citizens revolted forcing Susenyos out of office and ordering the Jesuits to leave the country. Jesuits did not obey this expulsion order so Apollinaris along with others were arrested, imprisoned in an Orthodox monastery and eventually hanged. (Ban, JLx, Som, Tan, Tyl)

Joseph M. Amiot
(French: 1718-1793)

Joseph M. Amiot

Joseph   was   a   missionary   to China   who   specialized   i n physics;   he   also   had   great talent   for   music.   He   mastered not   only   Chinese,   but   also   the Tartar   language   and   wrote extensively   about   the   state   of Chinese   science.   Joseph   had earned   the   confidence   of   the Chinese   Emperor   Kien-Long.

After   the   Suppression   of   the Jesuits   in   1773   Joseph   contin- ued   his   work   in   Peking   until his   death   with   the   support   of   the   same   French   government that   suppressed   the   Jesuits.   (Ban,   DSB,   Ham,   JLx,   Som)

Bl. Joseph Anchieta
(Canarian: 1533-1597)

Joseph   spent   most   of   his   life   as   a   missionary   to   Brazil   and eventually   became   the   *National   Apostle*   of   Brazil,   because he   is   a   co-founder   of   the   cities   of   Sao   Paulo   and   Rio   de Janeiro,   having   led   a   handful   of   Indians   from   their inhospitable   surroundings   to   settle   in   the   fertile   plains. While   young   he   dislocated   his   spine,   so   after   he   joined   the Jesuits   he   was   sent   to   Brazil   for   its   mild   climate   in   the   hope that   there   his   back   would   improve.   It   never   did,   however, and   he   was   in   pain   for   the   rest   of   his   life.   He   and Emmanuel   Nóbrega,   S.J.   arrived   at   the   village   of

Piratininga on the feast of St. Paul and so they named this mission São Paulo. For the next two decades Anchieta remained in the São Paulo district. There he completed a grammar and dictionary which were used by the Portuguese settlers and missionaries.

Joseph in the jungle

In 1553 he made his first contact with the Tupi Indians living on the outskirts of the settlement and since he was adept at languages and within a short time learned the Tupi-Guarani language of the Indians. Later Joseph was detained as a hostage by the menacing Tamoyo tribe and during these five months of loneliness and frustration, he occupied himself by composing a Latin poem in honor of the Blessed Virgin. Since he had no writing supplies he wrote in the wet sand and then committed the verses to memory. When he was released he set his poem down on paper: it had 4,172 lines!

Joseph succeeded in converting the Maramomis tribe and he wrote plays for his disciples to perform. These plays were written in different languages: Latin, Spanish, Portuguese, and Tupi. Because his dramas were the first to be written in Brazil Joseph is accorded the title *Father of Brazilian national literature*. In his letters he warned his successors that

In São Paulo 400th anniversary Mass honoring Joseph Anchieta

fervor was not enough for success in the mission: "You must come with a bag-full of virtues." This *wonder-worker of the New World* labored in Brazil for 44 years. (Ban, Ham, JLx, O'M, Som, Tyl)

John Andrés
(Spanish: 1740-1817)

John Andrés

John spearheaded a Spanish movement of literary criticism and was one of the world's first authors to trace out in broad lines a synthesis of all literary history. Though he never subscribed to any of Jean Jacques Rousseau's theological ideas, he admired his literary style and gave perhaps the clearest expression of the opinion the Spanish Jesuits had of Jean Jacques Rousseau. In his great work, the *Origin, Progress and Present State of All Literature*, Juan criticized Rousseau's *Nouvelle Heloise*, admiring the literary merits while censuring the moral and theological weaknesses. John continued his scholarship during the years of the Suppression and in 1804 when Naples allowed the re-establishment of the Society John gathered Jesuits together to continue the work which had been interrupted in 1773. (Ban, Ham, JLx, Som)

Bl. Jerome De Angelis

(Italian: 1568-1623)

Jerome De Angelis

Jerome went to Japan shortly after ordination, but because of navigation problems it took six years to arrive. During this brief interval much had changed in Japan's attitude toward the Jesuits, so Jerome was greeted by one of Japan's most terrible persecutions of the Christians. Xavier could boast some thousand converts to Christianity and Xavier's successor, Cosme de Torres, increased the number to 30,000 within the next 20 years. Since there were never more than nine Jesuits in Japan until 1563, the increment was very encouraging and Jesuits thought that Japan was their most promising mission. When Luis de Almeida arrived later he gained the reputation for the best understanding of the Japanese and he was esteemed by them for his many skills. He established several medical clinics and orphanages. After his arrival Jerome De Angelis spent 12 years working with the Nagasaki Christian population until the 1614 edict expelling all Jesuits and bringing an end to the Catholic missions in Japan. Jerome went into hiding in Nagasaki so he could continue to comfort the Japanese Christians during this terrible time. To conceal his priestly identity, he disguised himself as a merchant and continued to minister to his people. But eventually Jerome was arrested with 47 Christians who were all burned to death. (Som, Tan, Tyl)

Claudius Aquaviva
(Italian: 1543-1615)

Claudius served for 34 years as the fifth Superior General. At the age of 37 having been in the Society only 14 years he began the longest term of all 29 Generals. During his term the size of the Society almost tripled from 5,000 to 13,000. Claudius codified Jesuit educational methods and showed great concern about missiological questions such as the adaptation of the message of the Faith to the cultures of

Claudius Aquaviva

China, Japan and India. (Ban, Ham, JLx, O'M, Som)

Bl. Rudolph Aquaviva
(Italian: 1550-1583)

Rudolph was martyred in India on the orders from a village sorcerer who felt threatened by the impact Rudolph had on his villagers. Nephew of the fifth Jesuit Superior General, Rudolph Aquaviva had trouble convincing his family of his Jesuit vocation. Once he succeeded and finished his studies he was chosen along with two other Jesuits to go to India and explain Christianity to India's enlightened mogul, Akbar, who had already invited Zoroastrian, Moslem, and Brahmin theologians to discuss their creeds in his imperial court at Fatehpur. Aware that Rudolph for all his mildness was a suasive debater, Akbar cautioned him against offending the sensitivities of his adversaries. The theological discussion lasted for three months and Akbar showed genuine sympathy with Rudolph's position by publicly walking with him with his arm about Rudolph's neck. Akbar was, however, seriously troubled by the mysteries of the Trinity and the Incarnation, but the real stumbling block in accepting Christianity was his realization that he would have to give up his harem. Rudolph's hope for the mass conversion of India was not realized.

Rudolph Aquaviva and companions

After this he was called to become a superior in Salsette, south of Goa. It was during a visit to one of his mission stations that he was hacked to death by the jealous sorcerer's accomplices. (Ban, Ham, JLx, Som, Tan, Tyl)

St. Edmund Arrowsmith

(English: 1585-1628)

Edmund Arrowsmith

Edmund became a martyr in England. His parents were persecuted because they had refused to attend Protestant services and had even harbored priests in their home. As a layman Edmund had worked among the beleaguered English Catholics for 15 years in Lancashire. He was well loved because of his pleasant disposition, his sincerity and indefatigable energy. He was quite outspoken and so in 1622 when he was arrested and put into prison he brazenly argued religious questions with the local Protestant bishop. Of course it was to the advantage of Elizabeth's governors and hierarchy, who were living on confiscated Catholic property, to spread a distrust of Catholic priests as agents of Catholic Spain and also to nourish the fear of an imminent Spanish invasion. To keep all this in place Elizabeth had her own *Inquisition*.

Edmund was released from prison because of a pardon given by King James I. After making the *Spiritual Exercises* Edmund entered the Jesuits and returned to Lancashire for the remaining five years of his life. He was arrested again by the priest hunters and imprisoned on charges of being a priest. He decided to let the court do its duty and prove the charge rather than help them with a confession, replying: "Would that I were worthy of being a priest." As soon as the jury did find him guilty of being a Jesuit priest he exclaimed: "Thanks be to God." When he was brought to execution he prayed for everyone in the kingdom then said: "Be witnesses with me that I die a constant Roman Catholic and for Christ's sake; let my death be an encouragement to your going forward in the Catholic religion." (Ban, Cor, JLx, Tyl)

Edmund Auger
(French: 1530-1591)

Edmund Auger

Edmund was a Latin scholar and very effective preacher; in fact he is said to be "among the five greatest preachers of all time." It was he who initiated the remarkably successful tradition of suasive Jesuit oratory in France that brought Calvinists back to the Catholic Church in large numbers (40,000 to 70,000 according to the historian Alfred Hamy). In 1563 Edmund wrote a catechism to answer "the errors of our times", and in particular the teachings of Calvin. It was initially popular but since it was so polemical and theoretical, it was soon replace by the catechism of Peter Canisius. Edmund was friend, counselor and confessor to the French King Henry III who, in gratitude to Auger, gave the Society the beautiful *College de la Trinité*. Edmund started another tradition as the first of many Jesuit confessors to French kings. Upon his death he was given the title: *Père de la patrie*. (Ban, Ham, JLx, O'M, Som)

Ignatius
de Azevedo
(Portuguese: 1527-1570)

Ignatius and 39 martyrs

Ignatius was one of the *Forty Martyrs of Brazil* who met their deaths off the Canary Islands at the hands of Huguenot pirates. Ignatius had worked in Rome as procurator for India and Brazil, then the Superior General, Francis Borgia, assigned him to Brazil as *Visitor* to find how Rome could help the Jesuits working there. The answer was *more Jesuits,* so Ignatius went to visit the Spanish and Portuguese provinces of the Society to find volunteers for the Brazil mission. He succeeded in gathering 49 young Jesuit volunteers. In spite of the clear danger of pirate ships these 50 young men sailed off in two ships. Ignatius expressed his feeling: "If the Huguenots should capture us, what harm can they do? The most they can do is to send us speedily to heaven." On July 15, 1570 as they were heading into the Port of Palms, near the Canary Islands, one of the two ships, with 40 Jesuits aboard, was overtaken by five faster pirate ships under the command of a French Huguenot, formerly a Catholic and now a declared enemy of Jesuits. When the pirates boarded the ship and saw Fr. Azevedo in the center of the ship holding a painting of the Virgin Mary, a pirate slashed him with a sword as he protested: "You are my witnesses that I am dying for the Catholic Faith." The pirates picked up his body and hurled him overboard with the painting still held tightly in his hands. They then hacked to death the rest of the 39 Jesuits and threw them all into the sea, leaving unharmed the rest of the passengers. (Ban, Cor, Ham, JLx, Tyl)

stamp honors 40 martyrs

Jacob Balde
(German: 1604-1668)

Jacob Balde

Jacob was a Latin poet who served as sodality director and court preacher at Munich, Landshut and Amberg. He soon acquired a wide reputation as a n outstanding scholar and some contempo- raries called him a *Sec- ond Quintilian*. Jacob's numerous works of po- etry, written mostly i n Latin, were marked b y brilliant imagination, nobility of thought, tender affection, wit, knowledge of the human heart, and profound learning. He also wrote music and dramatic poetry, the most important of which is *The Daughter of Jephthah* which was frequently performed at Jesuit schools. His poems and other writings deal in ideas of the world in which he lived, ranging from religion, arts and letters, love of friends and of country, the virtues of patient endurance and fortitude. Over 70 odes honor the Blessed Virgin Mary. His patriotic poems, it is said, make him the German *poet for all times*. Jacob was a master of classical Latin and, like Horace, wrote four books of odes and one of epodes. Balde tried his hand at epic verse i n such poems as *The Battle of the Frogs and Mice* in five books and On the *Vanity of the World.* Among his satirical poems are found 22 poems on The *Glory of Medicine* and one *Against the Abuse of Tobacco.* (Ban, Ham, JLx, JLP, Som)

Daniel   Bartoli
(Italian: 1608-1685)

Daniel   Bartoli

Daniel   was   an   historian,   a physicist and a very effective mathematics   teacher.   He sought to link the speculative and   the   experimental   ap-proaches to science and did n o t hesitate to praise the works o f Galileo whose works were still on   the   Index   of   forbidden books. On the other hand h e was   not   afraid   to   criticize Galileo's   faulty   opinions   o n harmonic   motion.   J u d g i n g from the number of editions and translations of Daniel's works, his books were widely read, supplied many ideas f o r the scientific debates of the day and helped inculcate a n appreciation   for   scientific   evidence.   Daniel   wrote   a scholarly   meditative   work   of   philosophical   a n d astronomical interest, with curious notes on a diversity o f topics - flowers, the Pisa cathedral, atheists, church domes, hunting,   quicklime,   snails,   demons,   dissonance   in music, geometrical   proofs,   Leonardo,   Michelangelo,   t h e microscope, navigation, clouds, the eye, the cathedral f l o o r of Sienna, the doors of the Baptistry at Florence, the r u l e r s of Mexico, China and Persia, chess and sleep. His w o r k s were published in translation by Thomas of Salsbury, t h e translator   of Galileo's works, who used Daniel as a n example of a man pursuing scholarship in spite of p o v e r t y and   hostile   criticism.   Thomas   was   using   Daniel   as a n example to encourage   the appreciation   of original ideas and discourage the worship of authority. Daniel wrote a frequently quoted life of Ignatius Loyola for which he w a s still correcting   the proofs on the day he died. (Ham, JLx, Som)

John Bathe
(Irish: ?-1649)

John worked at the Jesuit college in Drogheda until the invasion of Cromwell when he was seized, taken to a public square, beaten, then shot by the soldiers of Oliver Cromwell. In the fall of 1649 Cromwell with 12,000 soldiers had surrounded the town of Drogheda and demanded that the Irish defenders surrender, promising that they would not be harmed. As soon as they put down their weapons all were killed by the British. Cromwell later justified the massacre of these 3,000 men on the grounds that this would strike terror into other Irish towns and would hasten future surrenders. He justified his further slaughter of the towns' non-combatants, women and children, in that they deserved to die because of past mob violence. Later another English patriot, Winston Churchill, no great friend of Ireland, had this to say about Cromwell's actions in Drogheda. (Ham, JLx, McR)

"There followed a massacre so all-effacing as to startle even the opinion of those fierce times. All were put to the sword. None escaped; every priest and friar was butchered. . . . Cromwell in Ireland, disposing of overwhelming strength and using it with merciless wickedness, debased the standards of human conduct and sensibly darkened the journey of mankind . . . Upon all of us there still lies 'the curse of Cromwell'."

Winston Churchill

St. Robert Bellarmine
(Italian: 1542-1601)

Robert   Bellarmine

Robert was a Cardinal and Doctor of the Universal Church and one of the most learned men of his time. His books were such a powerful vindication of the Catholic Church that Queen Elizabeth forbade her subjects from selling them under pain of death. A very popular orator, he could memorize an hour-long Latin sermon by reading it over once. He had the ability to simplify the great truths of theology and put them within range of ordinary people. He confronted the Protestant Reformers and justified the right of the Catholic Church to confront moral issues and to help guide and correct the temporal order.

Over Robert's protests the Pope made him a Cardinal "because he was without equal for learning in the Church of God." From this new vantage point he then set about to root out the abuses inside the Catholic Church which gave the Reformers grounds for their criticisms and presented to Pope Clement VIII a denunciation of the major abuses prevalent in the Pope's own Roman Curia. He pointed out that the Pope was not the Church's overlord but its administrator. Only Pope Sixtus V's death prevented Robert's writings from appearing on the *index of forbidden books* because Robert opposed the Pope's theory of *direct* papal power over civil authority. Galileo invited Robert to see the new-found wonders of the sky in his telescope and later Robert turned to Jesuit scientists to confirm Galileo's findings. This resulted in Robert's gentle treatment of Galileo at his famous trial - which leniency did not please the *Holy Office*. Robert, however, was not to be intimidated by anyone either outside or inside the Church. (Ban, DSB, Ham, JLx, O'M, Som, Tyl)

St. John Berchmans

(Belgian: 1599-1621)

John Berchmans

As a Jesuit scholastic (seminarian) John was noted for his good-natured disposition who "did nothing extraordinary, but did ordinary things extraordinarily well." He decided to become a Jesuit after reading the life of another Jesuit scholastic, Aloysius Gonzaga. John's father was a shoemaker and hoped that John would become a diocesan priest so that he would be able to help the family with a fixed income, but John was determined to become a Jesuit. During John's seminary days in Belgium the Jesuit General requested two Flemish Jesuits to work in the Roman College. John was chosen and with his companion set out on the 10-week journey, walking the entire 800 miles from Antwerp to Rome.

Hoping to serve the multilingual migrants overrunning the continent at that time, John resolved to learn all the principal languages of Europe and he demonstrated great linguistic ability. It was his desire to serve on the China mission after ordination. His performance in philosophy and science were so brilliant that he was assigned the arduous task of a "public defense" which meant that he had to prepare the whole field of philosophy and answer any questions posed by the faculty and visitors in a public demonstration. His health broke during these studies precipitating his death at the age of 22, thus ending his dream of preaching the faith in China. Immediately after his death many of the Roman laity familiar with his scholastic ministries began to venerate him as a saint. (Ban, Cor, Ham, JLx, Som, Tyl)

William Berthier
(French: 1704-1784)

William   Berthier

William was the editor of the renowned Jesuit periodical the *Journal des Trévoux*. A leading scholar, William was in a position to emphasize the weaknesses in the "Great Encyclopedia", edited by d'Alembert and Diderot which best articulated the materialistic and anti-ecclesiastical philosophy of life which was called the *Enlightenment Movement.* Initially William greeted the new publication and wished it well, then he suggested that the editors of the *Encyclopédie* indicate their sources and use quotation marks when directly citing other works. William pointed out that the first volume of the Encyclopédie contained over 100 articles which had been taken without acknowledgment from earlier works. In particular, he specified parts of the Encyclopédie that had been lifted directly from the writings of the Jesuit, Claude Buffier, who had died 15 years earlier. This revelation challenged Diderot's claim that he and his colleagues were pioneers in this research. William, however, remained open to the positive contributions of the authors. Determined to work for an understanding with the intelligentsia he supported their evident intellectual curiosity and their idea of recording human progress. But as more volumes were published along with an increasing number of serious flaws William sharply condemned the *Encyclopedia*. (Ban, Ham, JLx, Som)

Thomas Betagh
(Irish: 1738 - 1811)

Thomas Betagh

Thomas was an educator i n Dublin and founded a "free school" where 300 Irish boys, poor in everything but ability and spirit, received their education. He acquired desperately needed clothing for many of the students. After the Suppression of the Jesuits Thomas became the Vicar-General of the Archdiocese of Dublin and was known as a very vigorous pastor. The inscription on his marble monument in the Cathedral Church reads: "His chief delight and happiness was to instruct the young, especially the needy and the orphan." Thomas supported Daniel O'Connell's stand in opposing the other Irish bishops who wished to submit to a British scheme uniting Ireland with England, thus bringing them into the United Kingdom i n exchange for citizenship for all Catholics. The plan would give the English king veto power over any appointments of any future Irish Catholic bishops.   (JLx, Som)

An extra glimpse of the early Society

Part of a 1673 letter from St. Oliver Plunket, Archbishop of Armagh, victim of the Titus Oates plot praising the courage of the Irish Jesuits

Nicolas   Bobadilla
(Castilian: 1511-1590)

Nicolas was one of the first
companions of Ignatius Loyola. He studied rhetoric, logic
and theology in Valladolid. He
joined Ignatius in Paris, was
ordained in Venice and then
went to Italy where he
traveled through more than
70 dioceses as a preacher and
missionary. He worked also in
Germany and in Dalmatia.
Nicolas was sent by Pope Paul
III to help reconcile Juana of
Aragon with her husband. He

Nicolas   Bobadilla

was chosen to go to India at the request King John, but
because of his illness was replaced by Francis Xavier.
Nicolas had dealings with eight popes, three emperors,
numerous electors, German princes, cardinals and prelates
through all of Italy. He was a man of much talent and great
contrasts, independent and impulsive, outstanding for both
accomplishments and imprudence. The Pope kept him from
participating in Jesuit deliberations in Rome in 1539 and
1541, Charles V expelled him from Germany in 1548 and his
unsuccessful demands for modifications in the Society of
Jesus caused papal intervention. His work on frequent and
daily Communion was the only one of his works published
during his lifetime. Nicolas was the last of the original
seven Jesuits to die. (Ban, Ham, JLx, O'M, Som)

St. Andrew Bobola

(Polish: 1591-1657)

Andrew Bobola

Andrew suffered one of the most painful martyrdoms ever recorded. Andrew became an outstanding preacher and he directed Sodalities from which he recruited assistants to help him catechize, visit prisoners and the poor and assist plague victims. Andrew found that many of the Catholics living in Eastern Poland had become Orthodox simply because they had no Catholic church, so he built one and it soon became a center for all who wanted to return to the Catholic Faith. Two entire villages returned to the Catholic Faith through his preaching. Because of Andrew's success some of the Orthodox, supported by Cossacks were eager to annul such reunions and rid those territories of all Catholic churches. Because of Andrew's success they urged street ruffians to throw stones at him whenever he walked through a town. Andrew was quite aware that his martyrdom was not unthinkable. Then, in May, 1657 the Cossacks attacked Janów and massacred Catholics and Jews. They arrested Andrew and threatened him with torture unless he converted. He was unmoved, so the fanatical Cossacks took him to a butcher's shop, stretched him on the butcher's table, and flayed him alive. After two hours of this pain, during which he continually prayed for his tormentors, he expired. (Ban, JLx, Tyl)

John von Bolland
(Belgian: 1596-1665)

John was a Belgian theologian
and historian responsible for
the society named in his
honor, *The Bollandists*. This
Society of Bollandists was
started in 1603 by Héribert
Rosweyde, S.J. in order to produce critical editions of the
enormous number of manuscripts concerning the lives of
the saints which had accumulated in multilingual
European libraries. Jan suc-

John von Bolland

ceeded Rosweyde and approached the job in great earnest.
Later Pope Alexander VII praised this scientific
hagiography, perhaps with excessive generosity: "Never
had there been undertaken up to that time any work more
useful and more glorious to the Church." Bolland's work
was not without critics, which included the Spanish
Inquisition, because some treasured legends concerning
the saints were exposed as legends. The Carmelites found,
for instance, that their Order was not founded by the
prophet Elijah. Not considered a threat to the Church, the
Bollandists Society was able to survive the Suppression in
1773 but had to pursue a scaled-down schedule. After the
Restoration of the Society in 1814, the Bollandists were
moved to Brussels. The first two folio volumes of the *Acta
Sanctorum* each containing over 1,000 pages had been
printed back in 1643. Today in this *scriptorium* sanctuary
the Bollandists still research the lives of saints in order to
present to us as honest and clear a picture as possible of
the lives of those who are now with God. They can well
boast of one of the best historical libraries in Europe and
now have published over 100 volumes. Today the Bollandist
have their own World Wide Web with URL location:

http://www.kbr.be/~socboll/

(Ban, Ham, JLx, Som)

St. Francis Borgia

(Spanish: 1510-1572)

Francis Borgia

Francis had an unusual background for a Jesuit not only having a family and being the father of eight children but also of being the great-grandson of Pope Alexander Vl on the paternal side and great-grandson of Ferdinand of Aragon on the maternal side. It was the layman Francis who introduced Italian Renaissance styles of music to Spanish culture. Charles V made him viceroy of Catalonia and later he became duke of Gandia, but on the death of his wife he entered the Society of Jesus and became a friend and adviser of Ignatius of Loyola, who gave him the care of the missions in the East and West Indies. In 1560 he succeeded Laynez to become the Society's third Superior General. Concerned that Jesuits were in danger of getting too involved in their work, he introduced the daily hour-long meditation. Under his generalship the Society established missions in Florida, New Spain and Peru and greatly improved its internal structures, and for this Francis is sometimes called the *Second Founder of the Society of Jesus*. (Ban, Cor, Ham, JLx, O'M, Som, Tyl)

Roger J. Boscovich
(Croatian: 1711-1787)

Roger J. Boscovich

Roger was a physicist, geometer, astronomer and philosopher. Roger had an older brother, Bartholomew, who was also a Jesuit mathematician and on occasion taught in Roger's place when Roger was needed elsewhere. He taught at the Roman College for 20 years, although the Jesuit General Luigi Centurione, S.J. thought his teachings too avant garde. The next Jesuit General, Laurence Ricci, however, valued Roger and chose him as *Visitor* of the whole Jesuit Society. He was also a correspondent for the Royal Society of London, and a frequent contributor to the Jesuit *Mémoires des Trévoux*. The famous astronomer Joseph Lalande said there was no scholar in all Italy like Boscovich nor did he know any geometer as profound.

Roger developed the first coherent description of atomic theory in his work *Theoria Philosophiae Naturalis*, which is one of the great attempts to explain the universe in a single idea. His influence on modern atomic physics is undoubted. His legacy has been preserved in the special *Boscovich Archives* in the Bancroft Rare Books library at the University of California in Berkeley. Among the 180 manuscripts and 2,000 letters housed there are found many of his 66 scientific treatises as well as correspondence with the major scientists of his day. On the anniversaries of his publications, his birth, and his death, symposia are held throughout the world to honor this amazing polymath. Roger was a creative scientist credited with perfecting the ring micrometer and the achromatic telescope. He was the first to apply probability to the theory of errors according to Laplace and Gauss. It was his influence that minimized the hostility of Catholic churchmen to the Copernican system, and he had such a reputation for honesty, integrity and scholarship that only he was able to persuade Pope Benedict XIV to finally remove Copernicus from the *Index of Forbidden Books.*

After the Suppression of the Jesuits he became captain of optics in the French navy. Born in Ragusa (now Dubrovnic, Yugoslavia), Roger lived a long, fruitful life. Incisive in thought, adventuresome in spirit, and independent in judgment; he was a man of the 18th century in some respects, but far ahead of his time in others. A lunar crater is named to honor him. (Ban, DSB, Ham, JLx, Som)

Dominic Bouhours

Dominic Bouhours
(French: 1628-1702)

Dominic gained a reputation as one of the masters of correct writing of his time. He was among the first to develop the idea of *taste* which he treated in his famous "Art of Criticism: or the Method of Making a Right Judgment upon Subjects of Wit and Learning". Apparently because of Dominic's work, later literary critics focused more on general literary appreciation. He influenced Nicholas Boileau, Jean de La Fontaine, Jacques Bénigne Bossuet, Dryden, Addison and Lord Chesterfield. Jean Racine introduced Dominic's tragedies with the accolade: "You are one of the supreme masters of our tongue." (Ban, Ham, JLx, Som)

Louis Bourdaloue

Louis Bourdaloue
(French: 1632-1704)

Louis was a preacher for 34 years. His sermons reached classical perfection in their logic, structure and wealth of doctrine. In eloquence he ranked as one of the great master during the reign of Louis XIV and was called the "king of orators and the orator of kings." He preached five Lenten series of sermons and seven Advent series of sermons before the court. He was often invited to preach at ceremonies for all kinds of religious occasions. He emphasized the traditional doctrine of Church, which he explained and defended with great lucidity and was especially eloquent while speaking against Jansenism. Louis won for himself a high place in French literature: Fenelon said that his style "had perhaps arrived at the perfection of which our language is capable in that kind of eloquence." Voltaire was among many thinkers who referred to Louis as "One of the world's greatest speakers". (Ban, Ham, JLx, Som)

St. John de Brébeuf
(French: 1593-1649)

John de Brébeuf

John as a youth in Normandy suffered such poor health that it was doubted he would ever become a priest. Once in Canada, however, he found the harsh climate so wholesome that hardy Indian braves stood amazed at his inexhaustible powers of endurance and his ability to carry tremendous loads. He was called Echon which meant *the load bearer.* His massive size made them think twice before sharing a canoe with him for fear he would sink it. Brebeuf described the difficulty of learning the Huron language in one of his many letters back to France and advised those who felt they were called by God to New France: "You may have been a famous professor or theologian in France, but here you will merely be a student and with what teachers! The Huron language will be your Aristotle, and, clever man that you are, speaking glibly among the learned, you must make up your mind to be mute in the company of these natives." In another of his relations he described a native American game and referred to the curved stick they used as *la crosse* because it reminded him of a bishop's crosier (la crosse). According to histories of the game it was John de Brebeuf who named the present day version of the Indian game *lacrosse.*

By 1650 the Huron nation had been exterminated, and the laboriously built mission was abandoned for a while. But it proved to be "one of the triumphant failures that are commonplace in the Church's history." These martyrdoms created a wave of vocations and missionary fervor in France. It also gave new heart to the missionaries already in New France. Like the Iroquois, they had imbibed the courage of John de Brébeuf. (Ban, Ham, JLx, Som, Tyl)

St. Alexander Briant

(English: 1553-1581)

Alexander Briant

Alexander entered the Society while in the Tower of London awaiting execution along with Edmund Campion. Alexander was a friend of Robert Persons and was present at the death of Persons' father. He was finally arrested in Persons' house, taken to the Tower of London where, as Robert reported: "They kept pressing him under torture just to state where he had seen Fr. Robert Persons. He replied, 'You will never learn that from me; do whatever you can. I have seen him and I have lived with him and yet I will never tell you where.'"

From prison, Alexander smuggled out a letter to Robert Persons. The Jesuits had devised a cunning method of using invisible ink made of common orange juice. It was a letter of exceptional beauty, expressing his earnest desire to be admitted into the Society. His letter described such remarkable spiritual consolation during torture that he did not feel the pain. It was an experience described by other martyrs such as John Gerard. When the rack master threatened to make him a foot longer if he did not disclose the whereabouts of Robert Persons, Alexander laughed at him and defied him to go ahead and do it. Alexander spoke of the experience in a matter of fact way: "I was filled and replenished with a supernatural sweetness of spirit . . . cheerfully disposed and prepared to suffer and endure those torments . . . . Whether what I am relating be miraculous or no, God knoweth, but true it is that in the end of the torture, though my hands and feet were violently stretched and racked, I was without sense and feeling well nigh of all grief and pain." Alexander was accepted into the Society and after completing his novitiate in the Tower of London, was executed at Tyburn minutes after Edmund Campion. (Ban, Cor, Tyl)

St. John de Brito

(Portuguese: 1647-1693)

John de Brito

John is the Apostle of Madura, India, where he was martyred. When John volunteered for and was assigned to India, his mother Senora de Brito objected strenuously to the Jesuit Provincial, to the papal nuncio of Portugal and to the Jesuit Superior General in Rome. When the Portuguese royal fleet sailed in 1673, John was one of the 25 Jesuits it carried to India. During his time there John converted more than 10,000 Indians to Christianity. From the very start of his mission he familiarized himself with the complicated procedures of the Indian caste system and discovered that most Christians belonged to the lowest, most despised caste. In order for Christianity to have a lasting influence, de Brito realized that members of the higher caste must also be converted, so he established himself as an Indian ascetic a *Pandara Suami*. He lived apart as they lived, dressed in a saffron cloak and turban. John set up small retreats in the wilderness in southern India where interested Indians could visit him. In time he became an accepted Suami, his reputation grew and he converted many, among whom was a certain prince who was told to give up his wives. One of the wives, the niece of the rajah, took this less than graciously and had John arrested, but he was later released. Because of his success in converting many Indians to Christianity, the Brahmins, the highest Indian caste, sought to kill him. They were finally successful; the rajah's soldiers apprehended and imprisoned John and his Catechists and fettered them with heavy chains. The rajah then ordered that he be executed, not anticipating, however, what a good sport John would be. Reaching the spot selected for his martyrdom, he knelt down in prayer. The rajah's order was publicly read, and when the executioner hesitated to do his job, John encouraged him, "My friend, I have prayed to God. On my part, I have done what I should do. Now do your part. Carry out the order you have received." He did, and John's death only spurred on the efforts of the remaining Christians. (Ban, Cor, Ham, JLx, Som, Tyl)

Paschase Broet
(French: 1500-1562)

Paschase Broet

Paschase was one of the first ten companions of Ignatius along with Xavier, Laynez, Faber, Salmerón, Simon Rodriguez, Bobadilla, Jay and Codure. He was sent by Pope Paul III to Sienna and shortly after he arrived, reports came back to Ignatius of startling results from his retreats and sermons. One of the early problems of the Society was to obtain legal recognition for its corporate existence in France. Broët did not let the king forget the Jesuits and in 1560 King Francis II issued a decree recognizing the Jesuit Order.

Accompanied by Alfonso Salmerón, Paschase was sent as papal nuncio to Ireland by Ignatius at the request of Pope Paul III in 1542 to find out what kind of apostolate was possible there. Ignatius had originally planned to send Francis Xavier who may have discerned better the caliber and potential of the Irish people. Paschase, however, lacked this insight and sent such a gloomy prognosis back to Rome that no Jesuit apostolate began until two decades later. In the following centuries, however, the Jesuit Irish mission flourished in Ireland with, schools, colleges, parishes and Sodalities which were quite active in caring for the sick in times of Ireland's many plagues and "troubles". (Ban, Ham, JLx, O'M, Som)

Peter   Brumoy
(French: 1688-1742)

Peter   Brumoy

Peter   taught   rhetoric   and   humanities   at   Caen   and   taught   mathematics   at   the   college   of   Louis-le-
Grand.   He   had   a   strong   interest   in
drama,   however,   and   his   principle
work   was   *Greek   Theater*.   The   latter
was   criticized   by   Voltaire   for   being
too   classical,   in   fact   Voltaire   was
distressed   with   the   very   popular   and   widespread
presentations   of   Jesuit   theater   because   he   thought   that
they   put   too   much   stress   on   classical   drama.   (Ham,   JLx)

Ven.   Bruno   Bruni
(Italian: 1590-1640)

Bruno   and   Louis

Bruno   was   a   missionary   to
Ethiopia   and   was   one   of   the   last
two   to   be   martyred   there   along
with   the   talented   linguist,
theologian,   and   mathematician
Ven.   Louis   Cardeira.   The   Jesuit
mission   had   been   progressing
rapidly   with   the   help   of   the
Negus   Susenyos   who   had   become
a   Catholic   convert,   but   when   he
was   driven   out   by   the   Orthodox
Monophysites,   the   Jesuits   were
ordered   out   of   the   country   and   their   property   confiscated.
The   Jesuits   did   not   leave   and   were   captured,   imprisoned
and   then   hanged.   (Tan,   Tyl)

Tadeusz Brzozowski
(Polish: 1749-1820)

Tadeusz Brzozowski

Tadeusz taught the humanities at Minsk until the Suppression in 1773. Since the Tsarine did not promulgate the decree of Suppression in Russia, Tadeusz and others were allowed to continue teaching in their schools. In a very short time the Society had shrunk from 22,819 to 178 members. Tadeusz was a warmhearted man who had acquired a thorough knowledge of the Society's problems serving as secretary to the three previous superiors of the Society during the intervening years 1773-1814. Upon the Restoration of the Society in 1814 he was elected the 19th Superior General, the first General of the restored Society. (Ban, Ham, JLx, Som)

Philip Buonanni
(Italian: 1639-1725)

Philip Buonanni

Philip was a chemist, not only skilled in chemical analysis and experimentation but also familiar with the early publications on the nature of lacquer, some of which included the works of the Jesuit scholar, Athanasius Kircher. As a result of his studies conducted in Florence between 1690 and 1700, Philip was the first to publish an accurate and authoritative report on Chinese lacquer with applications to lacquer techniques in Europe. Philip concluded that Europeans would have to be satisfied with substitutes for the superior Chinese resin, since it could neither be shipped to Europe nor could its source, the Tsil tree, be cultivated in the western hemisphere. Philip's booklet was immediately recognized as a scholarly tract as well as a sound guide and his findings have been considered a milestone in the history of European lacquer because they ended the uncertainty about the differences between oriental and occidental ingredients. (Ham, JLx, Som)

Peter   Calatayud
(Spanish: 1689-1773)

Peter   Calatayud

Peter was called "The Xavier of Spain" because of the remarkable success of his spiritual apostolate among the many Spaniards who were indifferent to religion. He helped lift his country from spiritual malaise as he spread the retreat movement among the diocesan priests of Spain. Peter led a most austere and selfless religious life and was among the most popular preachers of the time. For 40 years he traveled throughout Spain giving missions which attracted thousands to the sacraments. When he was requested by a diocese to give a retreat to priests, it was so well received that more dioceses requested the same. This grew into a retreat movement, and soon he was preaching priests' retreats to more than 400 priests at a time. His deeply spiritual personal life helped make his efforts at spreading the new *Devotion to the Sacred Heart of Jesus* which caught fire among Jesuits as well as lay people, and soon became a centerpiece of the whole Jesuit apostolate in Spain. (Ban, Ham, JLx, Som)

St. Edmund Campion

(English: 1540-1581)

Edmund Campion

Edmund was a great disappointment for Queen Elizabeth because he twice turned down her generous offers of prestigious offices in the Church of England. This cost him his life. Born in London the son of a Catholic bookseller he would have entered his father's trade except for the fact that his bright wit earned him a scholarship to St. John's College, Oxford. He became a most sought after speaker and on one occasion so impressed Queen Elizabeth that she offered him a deaconate in the new state religion. He eventually fled to the continent, where he joined the Jesuit Order. After ordination he returned to London and there he wrote a *manifesto* of his mission which has come to be known as *Campion's Brag* in which he declared that his coming to England had a *religious* and not a *political* purpose. So direct, audacious and powerful was this *manifesto* that it was widely distributed to help encourage Catholics to remain firm in their faith. Eventually he was captured and taken to the Tower of London where he was stretched on the rack before his execution. After extended pain he was "hanged, drawn and quartered" and each quarter of his body was displayed on the four city gates. Many were very touched by the words in *Campion's Brag*: (Ban, Bas, Cor, Ham, JLx, O'M, Som, Tyl)

"And touching our Society, be it known to you that we have made a league - all the Jesuits in the world - cheerfully to carry the cross you shall lay upon us, and never to despair your recovery, while we have a man left to enjoy your Tyburn, or to be racked with your torments or consumed with your prisons. The expense is reckoned, the enterprise is begun; it is of God, it cannot be withstood. So the faith was planted; so it must be restored."

St. Peter Canisius
(Dutch: 1521-1597)

Peter Canisius

Peter was a renowned preacher, theologian, founder of many of Europe's schools and a Doctor of the Universal Church. Canisius was one of the *first* Jesuits, was the *first* Jesuit to publish a book, the *first* to found a university and the *first* Jesuit university president. He distinguished himself as a theologian at the Council of Trent and was considered *"the pride and ornament of all Germany"* and called *"the second Apostle of Germany"*. In 1550 he entered Germany with only two Jesuits; by 1580 their number had grown to 1,110.

Among the 37 books he wrote is his concise, lucid catechism which became a best seller, circulated in 15 languages. He was so pivotal in catechetical work that his name was synonymous with *catechism*. Centuries later one could still hear *"Have you learned your Canisius?"* Canisius found the effect of the Reformation on Catholics devastating. This calamity was apparent in an abysmal ignorance of the faith on the part of the laity as well as the clergy, whom he described as: "a scandal before God and the whole world." The more hopeless the situation seemed to be, however, the more energetic he became, stressing the need for education. He was instrumental in the founding of 18 colleges in as many cities with strong emphasis on academic excellence, insisting: "Better a college without a church than a college without a library." (Ban, Cor, Ham, JLx, O'M, Som, Tyl)

John Carroll
(American: 1735-1816)

John Carroll

John was born in Upper Marlboro, MD and was educated in Europe where he joined the Jesuits. After the Suppression he returned to Maryland in 1774 to live on his family's plantation in Maryland and there ministered to the people in what is now the District of Columbia. He was appointed superior of the American clergy in 1786, whereupon he decided to found an academy of the same quality that he had experienced in Europe. Thus Georgetown University was founded in 1789 (during the period of the Suppression of the Society) to supply intelligent Catholic laity for the young country. John was appointed bishop of Baltimore and gathered together fellow ex-Jesuits who formed the "Catholic Gentlemen of Maryland". Bishop Carroll had an enormous diocese to care for as well as his fledging academy with its own pioneering challenges.

John was two centuries ahead of his time, arguing for liturgy in the vernacular, for participation of the laity in running the church with interference neither by the state, nor by Rome in choosing American bishops. He later witnessed his *academy* firmly established by congressional action and the gradual increase of enrollment. At the end of his life he wrote of his satisfaction that, after the restoration of the Society of Jesus, more Jesuits would be joining this small school in years to come: "Everyone must acknowledge that the Society of Jesus rendered no service more useful than that of the education of youth. On this *academy* is built all my hope of permanency and success for our holy religion in the United States." (Ban, Bas, Ham, JLx, Som)

Joseph Castiglione
(Italian: 1688-1766),

Joseph and his dog

Joseph was a Jesuit Coadjutor Brother and a missionary in China, where he painted for the emperors at Peking and became a principal member of the Imperial Painting Bureau for 50 years. Joseph had composed some paintings in Genoa and then was sent to Peking. There he became known as *Lang Shinning,* a favorite artist and architect in the imperial court. He was active under three emperors: the grand K'ang Hsi, Young Caen and Ch ien Lung. The latter was an atrocious per-secutor of Christians, but his high esteem for Joseph afforded opportunity to the painter to intercede for his fellow Christians. Joseph brought with him a competence in European painting and was able to please his imperial patrons with *perspective* portraits, narrative accounts of imperial conquests, and studies of nature. His fusion of Western and Chinese elements may be seen in a wide hand scroll, about 30 feet long, representing 100 horses which is kept in the National Palace Museum, Formosa, and is said to have an almost surrealistic effect. He did this half a century before anyone in Europe would ever succeed in painting such complicated action. Another scroll, a painting about 25 feet long, is considered a true likeness of the Emperor, Ch'ien Lung. Joseph served also as architect for the Emperor's Summer Palace which gave the Emperor, Ch'ien Lung, his wish to have a Chinese equivalent of Versailles. Joseph is the only European painter recorded in the Chinese work *History of Painting,* composed of 72 chapters by P'eng Jun-ts'an about 1800.

For Joseph's 70th birthday the emperor sent a pro-cession to his dwelling together with a eulogy inscribed by himself. Upon the occasion of Joseph's death the emperor issued an edict which proclaimed: "Lang-Shih-ning (Joseph), who came from a foreign country, has been in service at the court since the reign of K'ang Hsi. He was diligent and careful, and the honor of the third degree had been conferred upon him. Now he has become sick and has died. In consideration of his many years of service and his advanced age of nearly eighty years, it is hereby ordered that he be given the rank of a vice-president of a Board and 300 ounces of silver for his funeral expenses, in order to show my special regard for him." His fellow Jesuits stated that: "With his art Brother Joseph promoted the cause of Christianity more than any one else had." A very high encomium coming from men who had known Ricci, Verbiest, Schall and other giants of the China mission. (Ban, JLx)

Commemorative stamp of Joseph's 100 horses

**More of Joseph's art
in Chinese stamps**

Nicholas   Caussin
(French: 1583-1651)

Nicholas   Caussin

Nicholas was a spiritual advisor to King Louis XIII, appointed by Cardinal Richelieu. Nicholas gave the reasons for his appointment: "The Minister of State, Richelieu, who appoints the king's confessor without leaving him any choice, looks for men who not only have the reputation of leading a good life, but at the same time are completely devoted to him. He now thinks that I shall be weak enough to tolerate evil deeds. But I will have no other care than to be as much use as possible to the Church and the public good . . . and to combat the evil deeds which the royal purple commits. Is not the harm done by the sins of monarchs, and the infection of their bad example, the greater in proportion as their position is an exalted one?" The sins which Caussin had in mind consisted in the king's following of Richelieu's counsels. These amounted to concluding alliances with Protestants and even with Turks, in order to make war on the Catholic empire of the Hapsburgs. In fiery indignation, Nicholas Caussin, in the year I637, gave an address to the king, and declared that the plans of the French government were absolutely detestable. This speech caused the dismissal of Nicholas Caussin from the court and Richelieu even imprisoned him as a political offender. After the deaths of Louis XIII and Richelieu in 1643, Nicholas returned to Paris, where he became confessor and spiritual director of a number of leading noblemen. (Ban, Ham, JLx, Som)

Thomas Ceva
(Italian: 1648-1737)

Thomas Ceva

Thomas was a geometer and carried on extensive correspondence with the famous mathematicians of his day. An essay of his appears at the end of one of the works of mathematician Guido Grandi, a Camaldolese monk. He invented a device to divide an angle into an arbitrary number of parts; 10 years later the device was claimed by L'Hospital, without any credit to Thomas Ceva. He brought Newton's theory of gravitation to Italy. Thomas was a poet also and his poem *"Jesus Puer"* (Milan: 1690) went through many printings, was translated into several languages, and occasioned many commentaries. In fact, Thomas has been considered one of the great Jesuit poets, despite the fact that he came from a famous mathematical family. "Ceva's theorem" is named for his brother Giovanni Ceva. (Ban, Bas, Cor, DSB, Ham, JLx, McR, JLP, O'M, Som)

Francis de la Chaize

(French: 1624-1709)

Francis de la Chaize

Francis was the most renowned of all Jesuit royal confessors. He served as spiritual advisor to King Louis XIV for 34 years, during which time he disagreed with the pope's view on the indirect power the papacy had on the temporal matters of the king. A section of Paris, a Metro station and Paris' most famous cemetery are all named to honor François. (DSB, Ham, JLx, Som, Tyl)

An extra glimpse of the early Society

In 1588 an unknown young scientist named Galilei Galileo wrote to Jesuit Christopher Clavius inquiring about a center-of-gravity demonstration. He expressed exuberant admiration for Clavius.

I prefer Your Lordship's (Clavius) judgment to that of any other. If you are silent, I shall be silent, too: if not, I shall turn to another demonstration. I know that with friends of truth like Your Reverence one may and ought to speak freely. Excuse my delight in dealing with you, and continue to grant me your grace, for which I supplicate you in every instance.

Peter F. X. Charlevoix
(French: 1682-1761)

Peter F. X. Charlevoix

Peter traveled widely, especially in America and in 1744 described his experiences in his book *The History and General Description of New France* which is still used for the study of Canadian origins. He also wrote of the Paraguay Reductions relating how the Jesuits had introduced into the settlements the Spanish custom of celebrating feasts with music and dances to help the Indians find greater joy in Christianity. He described their intricate and complicated dances, their games of chivalry, their ability to walk on stilts six yards high and also their expertise on a the tight-rope. He was especially pleased with their performances in the short dramas he wrote for them. (Ban, Ham, JLx, Som)

San Ignacio: One of the many Jesuit Churches which were built in Paraguay: one of the few still partially intact.

St. Peter Claver
(Spanish: 1580-1654)

Peter worked for 35 years helping to alleviate the sufferings of the victims of Cartagena's despicable slave trade. He referred to himself as "the slave of the slaves forever". His missionary vocation had been inspired by a Jesuit Brother, St. Alphonsus Rodriguez who urged him: "Your mission is to the West Indies. Why don't you go there and work for the Lord"?

Peter Claver

He did go. He went to Cartagena in Colombia and dedicated his energy to the poor people who had been shipped like cattle from Africa to Cartagena only to be sold to the highest bidder. It was said of him that he seemed to be everywhere at once because of the incredible speed with which he went about visiting the sick and instructing the ignorant, even in the scorching sun, drenching rain or biting wind which usually kept many of the inhabitants of Cartagena indoors. When the wretched slaves caught sight of him they clapped their hands by way of salute. Peter managed to convince the local authorities to issue a law that no new arrivals be baptized until they received adequate instructions. He then managed to use this law to delay their life of slavery by prolonging his catechism classes, much to the chagrin of the slave dealers. Peter also irritated the wealthy citizens who came to him for the sacrament of Penance and found that they had to wait in line along with the slaves. Many of his own community were decimated by the plague that was ravaging Cartagena. Eventually Peter was struck down and unable to continue his apostolate for the last few years of his life. When he died fervor seized the whole city to honor him as a saint. The Jesuit college was besieged by crowds who came to venerate his remains. Slaves came from all parts of the city and neighboring towns. He was later declared the Patron Saint of African missionaries. (Ban, Cor, Ham, JLx, Som, Tyl)

Francis Xavier Clavijero
(Mexican: 1731-1787)

Francis X. Clavijero

Francis was a Jesuit scholar who was quite familiar with Europe's latest advances in philosophy, science, and history. He excelled as a linguist, historian, philosopher, writer and teacher. He taught in the Mexican Indian schools with initiative and imagination and exemplified the finest of the Catholic Enlightenment in Mexico. Angered by Europe's disdain for native American culture, he wrote his authoritative *Ancient History of Mexico*, a painstaking portrayal of the culture of Aztec Mexico. This book distanced the intellectuals of Mexico from those of Spain. In the past Francis has been praised as an intellectual leader and is now interred in the National Hall of Fame in the Rotunda of Illustrious Men in Mexico City because of his influence in preparing the way for Mexican independence. (Ban, DSB, JLx, Som)

Com. stamp honoring Francis

Christopher Clavius
(German: 1538-1612)

Christopher   Clavius

Christopher was one of the earliest Jesuits, served as professor of mathematics at the Roman College for 45 years and during this time won the respect and friendship of virtually every significant astronomer/mathematician of his day. He was a life-long friend of Galileo. Clavius exerted a wide influence on the schools of Europe as well as China through his Jesuit pupils laboring there. The historian of science George Sarton calls him "the most influential teacher of the Renaissance." Pope Sixtus V said, and later historians have echoed the sentiment: "Had the Jesuit order produced nothing more than Clavius, on this account alone, the order should be praised." Later mathematicians such as Leibniz, co-discoverer of Calculus, became interested in mathematics by reading Clavius' works. His *Euclidis elementorum* became the standard text in the European schools and led to his being called "the Euclid of the 16th Century". This illustrious scientist was the one whom scholars and potentates would entrust the most sensitive scientific problems of the day. Clavius anticipated many mathematical developments, such as the decimal point, parenthesis, use of logarithms and the vernier scale.

It was Clavius who replaced the Julian calendar with today's *Gregorian calendar*. He found that a solar year could not keep up with the Julian year, which was 664 seconds longer than the year was thought to have been. In an 800 page book Clavius explained the principles and the rules needed to correct this error. He did this in a time of primitive mathematical tools when long division was an advance college-level course. Implementation of Clavius' plan was not an immediate and universal success. Of the many attempts to solve the calendar problem, a few were slightly more precise than Clavius', but required a thorough knowledge of astronomy to compute any date. Kepler, defending Clavius' simple plan, said: "After all, Easter is a feast, not a planet!". Joseph Scaliger, author of a competing plan, took the rejection of his plan less than gracefully and referred to Clavius as nothing more than a "German potbelly". Scaliger later, in a cheerier mood, acknowledged his esteem for Clavius saying: "A censure from Clavius is more palatable than the praise of other men". The Clavius calendar had a fate similar to the adoption of the metric system in America today. The populace became disoriented and windows were broken in the houses of the European Jesuits who were blamed for the change. The Orthodox Church saw it as a Roman intrusion (which it was), and Protestant countries were reluctant to accept any decree from a pope. England did not adopt Clavius' calendar until 1751, while Orthodox Russia would require the Bolshevik revolution before it adopted the Clavius calendar.

Clavius made the following observations about mathematical training necessary for Jesuits.

"Many a professor of philosophy has made no end of mistakes because of his ignorance of mathematics. Once a month scholastics should be gathered to hear original demonstrations of the propositions of Euclid. That the Society may be able always to have capable teachers of mathematics, a number of men fit and able to undertake such positions ought to be chosen and organized in a private academy for the study of mathematics so that they might support each other".

Some years later, faced with mounting scientific and political problems, Clavius' successor, Christopher Grienberger threw up his hands in despair and said: "If only Clavius were alive now! How I miss his counsel!" (Ban, DSB, Ham, JLx, O'M, Som)

S. G. Peter de Cloriviere
(French: 1735-1818)

Peter de Cloriviere

Peter entered the English Jesuit Province at Liège in France
and was professed the year o f
the Suppression, 1773. P e t e r
was as "tough as a pirate", s o
anticipating a period of Jesuit
absence, he helped o r g a n i z e
groups of Jesuits under the titles of "The Fathers of the Sacred Heart of Jesus", "The Society of the Heart of Jesus" a n d
"The Fathers of Faith". He w a s
not a man to accept punish-
ment passively, and so he i n -
vited one of his friends to p a r -
ticipate in a plot aimed a t
"evangelical vengeance," c o n -
sisting of offering up p r a y e r
for those leaders guilty of the "destruction" of the Society,
starting with the rulers of France. At the restoration of t h e
order, Peter, 80 years old, was the only survivor of t h e
suppressed French province. He had lived in Paris,
concealed in a cellar most of the time, during the w h o l e
period of the Revolution, but was imprisoned w h e n
Napoleon came into power and was incarcerated in t h e
Temple prison for five years. In 1814 at the restoration, h e
was entrusted by the Superior General of the order w i t h
the re-establishment of the Society of Jesus in France.
With the aid of the "Fathers of the Faith of Jesus" h e
enrolled a large number of novices and, during the f e w
years that elapsed before his death, Peter succeeded i n
establishing a new and vigorous Jesuit Province in France.
(Ban, Cor, JLx, Som, Tyl)

Bl. Dominic Collins
(Irish: 1567-1602)

Dominic Collins

Dominic was born into an illustrious noble family and given a superb education. He became a naval officer of superior quality in both France and Spain, then joined the Jesuits as a Coadjutor Brother. He went to help the beleaguered Catholics in England but was captured by the English bounty hunters. He was interrogated by Queen Elizabeth's deputy Mountjoy who had heard so much about the distinguished background of this naval hero that he took the occasion to try to convert Dominic to the Church of England and to make him an officer in the British navy. Dominic would have none of it and so was brought to the gallows at Youghal, where he gave a memorable exhortation to his fellow Irishmen who were present. "Our ancestors have given their lives in bold profession of their Faith. Now it is our turn to uphold that Faith to the last breath. It is in the defense of my faith that I wish to lay down my life." The English glared at this fearless man who was about to leave life with the same indifference he had left wealth and title. The Commandant, seeing the crowd swayed by one of their own compatriots, ordered him pushed off the ladder. Dominic was disemboweled and quartered. Then with mindless incongruity the English executioner held up Dominic's heart chanting the quaint formula: "God save the Queen." (Ban, Cor, McR, Tyl)

St. Claude de Colombiere

(French: 1641-1682)

Claude de Colombiere

Claude was the spiritual director of St. Margaret Mary Alacoque, a Visitation nun at a convent at Paray-le-Monial. In an apparition to her, Christ called Claude "My Faithful Servant and Perfect Friend". He also informed Sister Margaret that the Jesuits, with Claude acting as intermediary, would spread devotion to the Sacred Heart: "Go to My servant, Father Claude de la Colombiere, and tell him from Me to do all in his power to establish this devotion and give this pleasure to My Heart." So, on Friday, June 21, 1675, the first Feast of the Sacred Heart was celebrated privately by the priest and Margaret Mary. Both were to be apostles of the Sacred Heart, but each in a different way.

Claude was later sent to London, but with the Catholic Faith outlawed and the penalty of death set on those who practiced it, England was an impossible place for public devotion to the Sacred Heart. Claude, in disguise, secretly visited the persecuted Catholics and through private conversation and the confessional he taught them a fourfold means of honoring the Sacred Heart: adoration, love, imitation, and reparation. In 1678, when the bogus "Popish Plot," hatched by Titus Oates and his conspirators roused Protestants against Catholics, Claude was banished from England on a charge of conspiracy against the government. Claude's enemies knew he was innocent, but they wanted to be rid of this Jesuit who was winning Englishmen back to the Church which they themselves had abandoned. (Ban, Bas, Cor, Ham, JLx, Som, Tyl)

Bl. Ralph Corby

(Irish: 1598-1644)

Ralph Corby

Ralph was called "The Apostle" by the poor Catholics of England to whom he administered the sacraments for 12 years before he was captured by the English priest-hunters and brought to the Old Bailey prison. There he was tried, found guilty of being a Catholic priest and condemned to death. He was visited by ambassadors from Spain, Bavaria and France. Ralph along with another Jesuit, John Duckett, was hanged drawn and quartered. Before Ralph was born, his parents had been Protestants but converted to Catholicism. They found that they had to move to Ireland to avoid persecution. Ralph was not the only religious in his family: his two brothers became Jesuit priests, his father became a Jesuit Brother, his mother and two sisters became Benedictine Nuns. (Ban, Bas, Ham, Som, Tyl)

Many Jesuits were led through "Traitors' Gate" at the Tower of London

Bl. John Cornelius

(Cornish: 1557-1594)

John   Cornelius

John   Conor   O'Mahoney   whose
middle   name   was   latinized   to
Cornelius was   born   in   Cornwall
of Irish parents.   He was   expelled
from   Exeter   College,   Oxford,   for
maintaining   Catholic   beliefs.   He
was   ordained   a   diocesan   priest
and   determined   to become   a Jesuit.   There   was   a special   bounty
on John's head because   he   was   so
successful   in   bringing   people
back   to   their   Catholic   Faith.
Eventually   he was   betrayed   by   a
servant   and   found   concealed   in   a
priest-hole.   A *priest hole*   offered   precarious   protection
from   the   Queen's   bounty   hunters,   who   were   highly
motivated men, not   from   any   religious   conviction but   from
the   very   profitable   practice   started   by   King   Henry   VIII of
acquiring   and   keeping   property   confiscated   from
Catholics.   When   asked   whether   he   was   a Jesuit,   he
answered   that   he   was   "among   those   who   liked Jesuits".
During   his   imprisonment   John   made   more   converts   to
Catholicism.   He   was   interrogated   by   the   archbishop   of
Canterbury, then   tortured   on   the   rack   to   find   the   names   of
the   Catholic   households.   The   Catholic   laity   endured
persistent   harassment,   humiliating   treatment   and
frightening   brutality   at   the   hands   of   Elizabeth's   secret
police.   They   risked heavy fines, imprisonment, torture   and
the   painful   death   of   being   pressed   to   death   for   hiding
priests.   During   imprisonment   Jesuits had   worked   out   a way
of   communicating   with   friends   by   means   of   letters   written
in   orange   juice - which   could   be   decoded   by   the   receiver
when   the   paper   was   heated.   This   cunning   device (at least
more   cunning   than   the   jailers)   was   described   in John
Gerard's *Autobiography*, which   Graham   Greene   called   "as
exciting   as   a   novel".   During   his   interrogation   John
Cornelius   implicated   no   one.   He   was   absorbed   in   the
fulfillment   of his   aspiration   having   officially   taken   the
vows of the Society of Jesus   while in   prison,   shortly   before
he   was   hanged   drawn   and   quartered.   (Ban, Bas, JLx)

Giulio Cordara
(Italian: 1704-1773)

Giulio lived through the depressing years of the Suppression and was a friend of the Superior General Laurence Ricci. He was an historian and claimed that the latter was too gentle a man to cope with the fierce treatment of the Society at the hands of her enemies. Giulio felt that Ricci offered too little resistance to the methodical slanders organized by Catholic churchmen, whereas not an inch of ground should have been yielded. Ricci on the other hand thought that the only way to survive the storms was by means of silence and patience. Giulio was aware that this enmity in Rome against the Society was of the most virulent kind. Giulio was convinced that these Roman pockets of hostility rather than the pressure of the Bourbon courts accomplished the Suppression of the Society in 1773. (Ban, Ham, JLx, Som)

Giulio Cordara

Destruction of a Jesuit school during the Suppression of the Jesuits in Portugal

Francis Coster

(French: 1532-1619)

Francis Coster

Francis was received into the society by Ignatius who was impressed by Francis' wit and sense of humor. Francis taught astronomy and Sacred Scripture and was one of the great Jesuit Latin poets. He was delegate to three General Congregations, served as rector three times, twice as provincial of Belgium and once as provincial of the Rhine province. Once he had been insulted by Lucas Osiander, one of Martin Luther's followers, in an insipid anagram. One of his community, a mathematician-poet, Charles Malapert, answered the insult in an anagram on Osiander's name. The letters in the two men's names are rearranged to spell out the verses. Osiander's anagram reads: "You certainly are an African ass; (sic! that's sure.)". Malapert's answer reads: "You jackass, you can't graze here; go back to your thistles". Anagrams were immensely popular in the 17th century. Coster himself had written an essay to answer Osiander, and complained in the dedication that the eight theses that Lutheran Osiander was attacking had been published 20 years previously and that they were objectionable to Calvinists, but not to Lutherans. The full exchange is found in *Jesuit Latin Poets* by J. J. Mertz and J. P. Murphy. (Ban, Ham, JLx, JLP, Som)

Peter   Coton
(French: 1564-1626)

Peter   Coton

Peter was a spiritual ad-
visor to French kings. He
was given the position in
an unusual way. A pillory
had been placed in the
middle of Paris as a re-
minder of the suspected
Jesuit complicity in the
murder of Henry III.
After the Jesuits returned
from banishment, King
Henry IV demanded that a
Jesuit be kept at court as
security for the good
behavior of the whole
Society. Thomas Coton was chosen and was to remain
permanently at court at the king's disposal. By his
pleasant, polished ways, Thomas won Henry's good-will and
gained his confidence. It was not long before the king
asked Thomas to become his spiritual director. Soon after,
the king gave the order to have the insulting pillory
demolished as a clear mark of favor for the Jesuits. Because
of local opposition to Jesuits it was suggested that the
monument be pulled down at night, but Thomas insisted
that Henry was no "prince of darkness, but a king of
light", and his measures had no need to shun the light of
day. This argument so pleased the king that he immediately
gave orders for the pillory to be pulled down at high noon.
Thomas remained an influential advisor for several more
changes of rulers, and for a time gained support for a
French alliance with Spain. (Ban, Ham, JLx, Som)

Thomas   Cottam
(English: 1549-1582)

Thomas Cottam

Thomas was a convert from Protestantism who studied for the diocesan priesthood, then joined the Jesuits with the intention of going to work on the Missions in India. This was changed as soon as the opportunity opened for Jesuits to return to England and minister to the persecuted Catholics. While studying in Rome Thomas became ill and was sent north to Lyons for his health. There he was recognized by an English priest-hunter who befriended Thomas, found out about his plans to go to England and had him arrested and taken to the Tower where Campion, Briant and others were about to be martyred. Thomas languished in prison for five months while officials tried to induce him to return to Protestantism and beg the queen's mercy. He would only reply: "I will not swerve a jot from my Faith for anything even if I had ten thousand lives, I would rather lose them all than forsake the Catholic Faith." He was hanged, drawn and quartered and his limbs were cast into a vat of boiling water to prevent those present from collecting his relics. (Bas, Som, Tan, Tyl)

Philip Couplet

(Belgian: 1622-1693)

Philip Couplet

Philip was a missionary who sailed to China with Ferdinand Verbiest in 1656, where he accumulated a great deal of information about Chinese customs, language, history and literature. He was sent back to Europe to get support for the mission, but on the way back to China drowned at sea somewhere near Goa. It is ironic that he had once told a fellow missionaries, who also was to die later in a shipwreck, that of the 600 Jesuits selected for the China mission in the century since Ricci's arrival in China only about 100 arrived at their destination. Thieves, pirates, sickness, shipwreck and storms took the others. He knew what he was taking about having published a catalog with the names and a *curriculum vitae* of each Jesuit who worked in China during that century. (Ban, Ham, Som)

S.G. Anthony Criminali

(Italian: 1520-1549)

Anthony Criminali

Anthony was the first martyr of the Society of Jesus, dying in India at the age of 29. He had been assigned to work along the fishery coast of India near Malabar by the mission superior, Francis Xavier. Contrary to the advice of Anthony, the Portuguese governor had established a tollgate to collect fees for the Hindu pilgrims. When the infuriated Hindus broke through the barrier, the Portuguese fled, leaving the small Christian village to absorb the furious Hindu hatred of Christianity. Anthony along with all the other Christians was clubbed and beheaded. (Ban, JLx, Som, Tan, Tyl)

An extra glimpse of the early Society

After meeting in Rome with the Jesuits on their way to the Chinese mission, Leibniz started a correspondence with them and sent a suggestion for explaining the Holy Spirit as part of the Trinity to the mathematically minded Chinese. He suggested using the analog to the square root of minus one as a sort of intersection of number and non-number. Leibniz was inspired by the work of another Jesuit Athenasius Kircher attempting to find an alphabet of thought which would enable all to speak of the creation of knowledge. Leibniz also wrote to Bernoulli in 1703, attributing his original interest in mathematics to the writings of Jesuit mathematicians Clavius, Gregory St. Vincent and Guldin.

Francis Desbillons
(French: 1711-1789)

Francis Desbillons

Francis was an accomplished Latinist and a poet who taught humanities and rhetoric at the Jesuit colleges of Nevers, Bourges, Caen, La Flèche and for 32 years at "Louis the Great" College in Paris. In the face of the Suppression of the Society of Jesus and the various pressures put to bear upon its former members, Francis accepted Count Palatine Karl Theodore's invitation and moved to Mannheim on the Rhine in 1764. He brought with him his considerable library (23,000 volumes), which became the nucleus of the college library at Mannheim. Francis is most famous for his fables and some of his contemporaries referred to him as the "Latin La Fontaine". A major work was a collection of *Aesopian Fables* published in various editions until the 1768 version in 15 books to which Desbillons added some 170 of his own fables to those of Aesop, Phaedrus, and other fabulists. A lasting contribution in the area of ascetical theology was Francis' edition of the Latin text of the *Imitation of Christ*. Some of his personal anguish and sadness at the Suppression of the Society of Jesus in 1773 is seen in his late works, *Exiled Bird*, *The Art of Being Well*, and *Poem on Christian Peace*. (Ham, JLx, JLP, Som)

Jeremias   Drexel

(German: 1581-1638)

Jeremias   Drexel

Jeremias was a Jesuit educator, preacher, and spiritual writer. A Lutheran by birth, he was converted in his youth, educated by the Jesuits, and then entered the Jesuit Order. He taught the Jesuit seminarians at Dillingen and then for 23 years was preacher at the court of Maximilian, the elector of Bavaria. It is said that his voice was strong enough to be heard in every corner of the church and that his sermons were such that an hour would seem like a few minutes. He accompanied Maximilian on his Bohemian campaign. Jeremias wrote some 20 works that were widely read and translated. His first work, *De aeternitate considerationes*, concerned various representations of eternity. Another of his works, *Heliotropism,* discussed man's recognition of the divine will and conformity to it. (Ban, Ham, JLx, Som)

An extra glimpse of the early Society

In his book *God and Nature* David Lindberg describes an early attempt to develop an accurate pendulum by one of the outstanding astronomers of the 17th century, the Jesuit, John Baptist Riccioli, S.J. John once persuaded nine of his fellow Jesuits to count 87,000 oscillations over the course of a day, enabling him to identify an error of three parts in a thousand. Lindberg was fascinated by this collaboration and observed that: "It is instructive to remember that it was [this Jesuit] Riccioli - not Galileo - who first accurately determined the rate of acceleration of a falling body."

Joseph   Eckhel
(Austrian: 1737-1798)

Joseph   Eckhel

Joseph became custodian of the imperial cabinet of medals for Austria's Maria Theresa. Joseph created new methods of classifying coins which helped the development of the science of numismatics. He also was brought to Florence to classify the grand duke's impressive collection of coins. After the Suppression Joseph was made the director of Vienna's imperial treasury and also professor of antiquities and archeology at the university. (Ban, Ham, JLx, Som)

An extra glimpse of the early Society

In 1956 in a speech at Loyola University in Los Angeles during an anniversary celebration of motion pictures, Cecil B. DeMille spoke of the 17th century Jesuit polymath, Athanasius Kircher, S.J. "The real pioneer of the movies is a Jesuit, Athanasius Kircher, S.J. who invented the magic lantern in the 17th century. It is interesting to note that this same Fr. Kircher was the first European scholar to call attention to the importance of Egyptian hieroglyphics."

Antonio Escobar de Mendoza
(Spanish: 1589-1669)

Antonio Escobar

Antonio taught and wrote on moral theology. He summed up the doctrine of Probabilism: "For, although the opinion supported by stronger grounds is more perfect and certain, no one is required to follow what is more perfect and certain, for the reason that, as it is impossible to arrive at absolute certainty, God does not demand it. God demands of us only that we should act with such moral certainty as is to be found in the probable opinion. It would be an intolerable burden and would cause endless scruples if we were, in fact, to be bound always to follow the more probable opinion." This Probabilist theory was the target of Pascal's malicious attacks and provocative selection of quotations in his *Provincial Letters*, which led Pope Alexander VII to condemn some principles of the theory, although no pope ever condemned Probabilism itself.

In fact Antonio's moral theology book seems to have been the only Jesuit book Pascal ever read. Pascal's *Letters* were in no way representative of Jesuit works on morality, but his attack on Escobar were so vicious and memorable that Escobar's name became part of the French language meaning *prevaricator*. Voltaire praised the excellence of Pascal's *Letters* as literature, but was convinced that: "The whole book rested on a false basis. The author skillfully ascribed to the whole of the Society the extravagant ideas of a few Jesuits from whom many other Jesuits had differed."

The political powers of Europe, too, began at that time to pay some attention to these moral doctrines since the influence of the Jesuits in affairs of state had in many cases become extremely important. For instance, Escobar had taught that it is morally permissible for the subject to refuse to pay a tax which, according to a probable opinion, is unjust. So not only the irate Pascal but also the civil authorities, concerned about their national revenues, railed against Probabilism and against Antonio Escobar. (Ban, Ham, Som)

Philip Evans
(English: 1645-1679)

Philip Evans

Philip worked for 40 years in southern Wales, part of the English Mission. There he became known for his zeal and charity and enjoyed great popularity and success. Though he was especially pursued by those behind the Titus Oates plot Philip proved himself fearless. Over and above the usual 50 pounds for any Jesuit, 200 more were offered for Philip. Instead of fleeing the country, he stayed to serve the Catholics in Wales and was eventually caught. Refusing, of course, to take the oath of supremacy which recognized the king as supreme in all religious matters, Philip was imprisoned and hanged. (Ban, Bas, Ham, Tyl)

St. Peter Faber

(French: 1506-1546)

Peter Faber

Peter was a First Companion of Ignatius and was sent to give the Spiritual Exercises in Parma occasioning the return of many people back to the sacraments. Some even settled inside Peter's house waiting to go to confession. Ignatius once said that Peter Faber understood the Exercises better than anyone he knew. St. Alphonsus Rodriguez attributes his interest in the Jesuits to Peter Faber as does St. Peter Canisius, who as a young student traveled from Cologne to Mainz to consult with this famous Jesuit reformer about his vocation and to make the Spiritual Exercises. Faber's persuasive sermons brought thousands in Germany back to the Faith. In fact Melancthon left Cologne for good because of Peter's skill in public argumentation. From Germany Faber was sent to Portugal and Spain. King John of Portugal wanted to have Peter sent as Patriarch to Ethiopia, but Pope Paul III chose him to serve as his own theologian at the Council of Trent.

Peter was considered the most "ecumenical" of the early companions. At the very moment of Peter's death, Canisius was expecting from him an apostolic plan for Germany. Laynez, requested by the Republic of Venice to do something about Protestantism in Brescia, came to solicit Peter's advice. Peter wrote for his companions a series of guidelines on how to deal with Protestants. If Peter and others had been allowed to put these guidelines into practice there would later have been much less antagonism between Protestant and Catholic. Peter's guidelines come down to a few general attitudes and some practical suggestions, especially for contacts with individual Protestants. The first was to be careful to regard them with charity. Peter calls for a genuine spiritual conversion, essential to ecumenism and in need of constant renewal. Peter said: "It is necessary to win them over so that they will love and esteem us in their hearts. This can be done by speaking familiarly with them on subjects we have in common and by avoiding debates in which one side wins out over the other; for we should talk about things which unite us before taking up things which give rise to differences of opinion." (Ban, Cor, Ham, JLx, O'M, Som, Tyl)

Honoré Fabri
(French: 1607-1688)

Honoré   Fabri

Honoré wrote more than 30 works, many of them on scientific topics, some of which were reviewed in the *Philosophical Transactions*. In his treatise *De Homine* Honoré presents discussion of the circulation of the blood. Sommervogel implies that Fabri discovered it without knowing of Harvey's work on the subject. Honoré was a member of the *Holy Office*. So when he stated his opinion that the Catholic Church would adopt a figurative meaning to the offending biblical passages if it was shown that the earth does indeed move around the sun, Pope Alexander VII was so upset that Honoré was thrown into prison for 50 days. Even then he was released only because King Ferdinand intervened. (DSB, Ham, JLx, Som)

John de la Faille
(Belgian: 1597-1654)

John taught mathematics at the Imperial College. He is the subject of a well-known painting of Van Dyke exhibited in the Brussels *Plantin Museum of Fine Arts;* it was on loan to the New York Metropolitan Museum in 1984. Since John was the tutor of Don Juan of Austria, he went on the latter's campaigns, and met his death during one such battle. (DSB, JLx, Som)

John de la Faille

The Frontispiece from the chapter on Jesuits working in Europe from Mathia Tanner's 1675 book *Societas Jesu* concerning 321 of the Jesuit martyrs killed during the first century of the Society's existence: 1540 to 1646

Juan Fernandez

(Spanish: 1526 -1567)

Arrival of Juan and Francis Xavier

Juan was a wealthy young man con- cerned about the latest fashion until a sermon by the Jesuit Francisco Estrada changed his changed his whole perspective on life leading him to join the Society as a Coadjutor Brother. He went to India where he became the companion of Francis Xavier as Francis left the Indies for his work in Japan. Juan was fascinated by Japanese culture and learned the Japanese language quickly. In a few years he was able to act as interpreter, and composed a Japanese grammar and lexicon. It is from Juan's letter that we know many of the details of Francis Xavier's extraordinary life.

In the *Museum of the 26 Martyrs of Nagasaki* hangs the original of the picture above showing Francis Xavier and Juan Fernandez arriving in Japan on their way to see the emperor. Francis soon realized that Japan's emperor was not only inaccessible, but also ineffective. So he and Juan visited the genuine power, the daimyo of Yamaguchi who received them most cordially and gave them a place to live and permission to preach. Juan did much of the preaching in place of Francis who never really learned Japanese. In two months the converts numbered 500. (Ban, Som)

Ven. Roger Filcock
(English: ?-1601)

Roger Filcock

After his ordination Roger petitioned to be sent on the English Mission. In a short time he was arrested, committed to Newgate Prison and convicted even though no witnesses had been produced. He suffered death at Tyburn, with a noble fellow-martyr and friend, the widow, Mrs. Anne Line (later to become St. Anne Line). Roger was Anne's confessor and often had celebrated Mass in her home. On one occasion Anne had invited a large number of Catholics to her home for Mass to be celebrated by the Jesuit Francis Page; the gathering aroused suspicion among the neighbors. The priest hunters were summoned and Anne delayed them long enough to allow Francis to escape. She was arrested and charged with having harbored a priest. At her trial, when asked if she was guilty of the charge, she replied in a loud voice for all to hear, "My lords, nothing grieves me more but that I could not receive a thousand more priests". Anne was sentenced to death along with Roger Filcock. She was canonized as one of the 40 Martyrs of England and Wales in 1970. (Bas, Jlx, Tyl)

The 40 martyrs: Anne is on the left with the white apron

Henry   Garnet
(English: 1555-1606)

Henry   Garnet

Henry   was   the   superior   o f the   English   Jesuits   and   w a s arrested   on   the   occasion   o f the   Gunpowder   Plot,   a mindless   plan   by   some   e x - treme   Catholics   to   blow   u p Parliament.   Henry   knew   o f the   plot   through   the   c o n - fessional   and   so   could   n o t reveal   anything.   He   w a s tried   for   treason;   he   was   sent to   the   gallows   because   h e would   not   break   the   seal   o f confession   which   was   a meaningless   concept   to   t h e civil   authorities.   (Ban,   Bas, Ham,   JLx,   Som,   Tyl)

An   extra   glimpse   of   the   early   Society

In 1669 King Charles II felt he needed a sundial for his garden in Whitehall: it had to be the best dial possible, so the Jesuit physicist Francis Line was chosen for the job. Some sort of gentleman's truce was arranged between the Jesuit prey and the English predator. Line built the dial himself, modeling it after a sundial he had built at Liege, and it was an immense success. Then this wanted Jesuit described it in   Protestant England's very own periodical, the *Philosophical Transactions of the Royal Society* (TRS, **23**, pp. 1416-1418), and published an illustrated book with the elaborate title:

An Explication of the Diall sett up in the King's Garden at London, an. 1669, by which besides the hours of all kinds diversely expressed, many things also belonging to Geography, Astrology and Astronomy are by the Sunne's shadow made known to the eye (Liege, 1673).

St. Thomas Garnet

(English: 1574-1608)

Thomas Garnet

Thomas was canonized in 1970 along with 39 other martyrs killed during the terrible persecutions of Queen Elizabeth. Because Catholic institutions of higher learning had been confiscated and turned over to Protestants who were aggressive advocates of the established religion, young Thomas went to the continent in 1593 to attend the newly opened Jesuit college at St. Omer in London. Because of a Channel storm he and his student companions were captured by the English Navy who tried to force them to accept Elizabeth's religion. They managed to escape and later Thomas returned to England as a Jesuit. His uncle, Henry Garnet, superior of all Jesuits in England, was in charge of the entire network of priests working secretly among the Catholics who had refused to take the Oath of Supremacy. Thomas Garnet labored near Warwickshire for six years until his ministry came to an end with the discovery of the Gunpowder Plot.

The Jesuit martyrs of this time were known for their intelligence, joy and humor as well as for their deeper understanding of martyrdom as apostolic, noting that: "The gallows is the best pulpit anyone could ever preach from". Thomas even asked his superior to dissuade those who were planning to secure his escape from jail and martyrdom. (Ban, Bas, Cor, Ham, JLx, Som, Tyl)

Bl. John Gavan
(English: 1640-1679)

John Gavan

John was one of the martyrs whose death at Tyburn was occasioned by the Titus Oates plot which caused death and sufferings for hundreds of innocent people. None of these Jesuits was particularly distinguished except in bravery and innocence. At the time a number of apostate priests had turned informers. One such was John Travers who had had a dispute with his religious superior over money and was dismissed from the Jesuits. He appeared as a witness in the Oates Plot, under the name "Savage" and sought to involve men against whom he nursed grudges.

John Gavan was an eloquent man who was an accomplished preacher and tireless worker. At his trial at the Old Bailey he defended himself and four Jesuit companions quite convincingly, but to no avail; his arguments were ignored. At one point he tried to stifle a long-winded Lord Chief Justice, "Pray my Lord, let me speak, or else, as I live, innocent men will be lost". John's ingenuity startled the courtroom when he suggested that the judge might as well go back to the medieval practice and let him prove his innocence by the "trial by torture". Shortly after he was executed with four other Jesuits on 20 June, 1697. (Ban, Bas, Cor, Ham, JLx, Tyl)

Ven. Abraham George
(Syrian: 1563-1595)

Abraham George

Abraham was the first of the eight Jesuit Martyrs of Ethiopia. He was a Maronite Christian born in Aleppo, studied at Rome, then entered the Jesuits. After his ordination he requested to go to the missions and so left Rome for Lisbon to embark for India. It was while he was in Lisbon that Abraham learned through a spiritual experience. that he was to be martyred. Abraham arrived in Goa, India, and for a short time worked among the Saint Thomas Christians. From India he set out for Ethiopia even though its rulers still refused to permit Catholic missionaries to proselytize in their lands. Abraham disguised as a poor merchant, set out for the small island of Diu in the Red Sea, where he hoped to bring spiritual comfort to Catholics who had been without a priest for many years. Just a few months after his arrival, Abraham was arrested by the Turks, and was put to death by the sword. (Cor, Ham, JLx, Som, Tyl)

Bento de Goes
(Portuguese: 1562-1607)

Bento de·Goes

Bento undertook one of the greatest explorations in history in search of the fabled Kingdom of Cathay with its ancient Christian community reported by Marco Polo. After 4,000 miles and three years he found no Christian community but ended his journey at the Great Wall of China in 1605 proving that the Cathay of Marco Polo was the China of Matteo Ricci. Born in the Azores he became a soldier and traveled to Goa in India, where he entered and then left the Society of Jesus. Admitted a second time as a Coadjutor Brother, he volunteered for the mission to the Great Mogul and befriended the emperor Akbar. In quest of the kingdom of Cathay, he traveled the Silk Route through Central Asia and reached the outskirts of Beijing. Bento traveled disguised as an Armenian merchant named *Abdullah Isai* bringing rich gifts to offer to princes whom he should find on the way. After he passed through the Great Wall of China Bento sent a message to Matteo Ricci who sent a Chinese Christian to find him. He found Bento dying, perhaps from poisoning, and robbed of everything except a few notes about his fabulous three-year journey of 4,000 miles. Bento, however, had proven that there was no practical overland route between India and China, and no found sign of any Christian community in that part of the world. Bento de Goes is remembered as an illustrious missionary and explorer. On the occasion of his third centenary his native town, Vila Franca do Campo, erected a monument to him. (Ban, DSB, JLx, Som)   **Statue of bento in Vila Franca   ->**

St. Aloysius Gonzaga
(Italian: 1568-1591)

Aloysius in court

Aloysius died while attending the sick during the 1591 Roman plague. He was still a young Jesuit scholastic (not yet ordained). This young nobleman had repudiated the allure of Renaissance life and gave himself with powerful single-mindedness to the Ignatian ideal. In calling himself *"a piece of twisted iron that needed to be straightened out"* he was referring to his appalling background, of both his heredity and his environment. His ancestors included despots who condoned assassination, debauchery and extortion. They survived one assassination after another while their subjects were bled white by taxation. The Gonzaga princes alternated insane orgies with explosions of genuine underlying faith. Aloysius had a remarkable toughness of character; he was never a recluse and his innocence was founded on neither ignorance nor prudery. He could control quarreling princes and lead Roman rabble to confession. Aloysius had often helped his father, a reckless gambler, settle his debts. But in 1588 such a feud broke out in the Gonzaga clan that an army of lawyers and ecclesiastics could not solve it. It fell to Aloysius as the only one honest, imperturbable and clear-headed enough to settle the feud. Aloysius had hoped to be sent to work on the missions but while helping the victims of the plague, he contracted the plague and died at the age of 23. Usually known as the Patron Saint of Youth, this catechist of Roman ragamuffins, consoler of the imprisoned, martyr of charity for the sick, just as appropriately and deservedly could be honored as a Patron Saint of the Social Apostolate. (Ban, Cor, Ham, JLx, Som, Tyl)

St. Roch Gonzalez
(Paraguayan: 1576-1628)

Roch Gonzalez

Born in Paraguay, Roch was one of the main architects of the Jesuit *Reductions* there. It was through his work and work of men like him that made the Paraguay reductions such an amazing success both spiritually and economically. Realizing the damage of the slave trade, the Jesuits gathered the indigenous Indians and went inland away from Brazil. They came to Paraguay in 1609, built settlements for the Indians and taught them agriculture, architecture, construction, metallurgy, farming, ranching and printing. There were presses in the settlements for the school texts as well as for literature and art. This Utopia was suddenly destroyed by the avarice of the slave traders who were able to influence the Spanish crown. By the time the Jesuits were expelled in 1767, they had 57 settlements with 113,716 natives.

Roch belonged to the first generation of Jesuit Latin Americans who contributed so much to the human and Christian formation of their compatriots. Serving as a doctor, engineer, architect, farmer and pastor, he supervised the construction of churches, schools and homes and introduced care for cattle and sheep to the natives. To convert the simple Indians to Christianity, he skillfully adapted his lessons to their love of ornament, dancing, and noise. On the greater feasts of the Church Roch gathered the natives outside their small, straw-thatched church. Mass was celebrated outside with all possible solemnity, and for the rest of the day the Indians were treated to entertainment. In the large square, decorated with rainbow-colored tapestries, silks and feathers, there were games, bonfires, and religious dances.

To satisfy the natives' love of noise, Roch produced music of flutes and ear-splitting fireworks.

Com. stamp of Roch

In the four years he remained at St. Ignatius, the first of the Jesuit Reductions, Gonzalez saw his strenuous efforts meet with consoling success. Fierce savages, softened by Roch's gentle kindness, laid aside their hatred for religion and eagerly embraced the faith; vengeful natives, hearing him speak of peace, stifled their desire for revenge and made friends with their former enemies; timid women found refuge in the invincible courage with which Roch faced every threat and every danger; Indians, dying in horrible agony, were calmed by Roch's words as he prepared them for the end. In Roch the Indians found a staunch protector of their freedom. Greedy Spaniards, with an eye for easy money, craftily strove to lure the natives away from the Reduction and sell them into slavery, but ran against a stone wall in this indomitable man, Roch. He pleaded the Indian cause so forcefully with the Spanish Government that the Reduction of St. Ignatius was finally left in peace. Because of his success in Christianizing the natives, a local witch-doctor who was losing his control of the natives, martyred Roch along with his two Jesuit companions one day just as they finished celebrating Mass. (Ban, Cor, JLx, Tyl)

Melchior Grodecz

(Polish: 1584-1619)

Melchior Grodecz

Melchior was one of the three *Martyrs of Kosice* put to death at the hands of fanatical Calvinists along with Jesuit Stephen Pongrácz and Mark Crisinus, who was the Cathedral Canon in Kosice. Melchior taught and preached in Prague. During the 30-Years' War, however, as Jesuits were driven from one place to another, Melchior's journeys through Moravia and Slovakia finally led to his martyrdom when he arrived in Kosice, Hungary where he went to help fortify the Catholics there. A Calvinist prince in Transylvania was taking advantage of Hungary's war involvement and moved to expand his territory. At the time Kosice was a stronghold of Hungarian Calvinists, and the few Catholics who lived in the city and its outlying districts had been without a priest for some time. Melchior came to help the Polish speaking Catholics and Stephen Pongrácz came for those who spoke a Slavic language or German. When the Calvinist Minister heard the Jesuits had arrived, he sent his soldiers to arrest them. Melchior, Stephen and Mark were brutally burned, dismembered and then beheaded. The Calvinists refused to allow the Catholic citizens to bury their remains until three months had passed. Tenacious as were the Calvinists in their hold on some quarters of this unhappy country, they could not halt the creation of a powerful Catholic bastion there. (Ban, Cor, Ham, JLx, Tyl)

Joseph   Gumella
(Spanish: 1686-1750)

Joseph   Gumella

Joseph spent 35 years amidst the natives and the flora and fauna in the vast area of the Oronoco River in Venezuela. His 1741 publication of his floral specimens and botanical and ethnographic observations was a pioneer effort. Under his care a village flourished due to his clever craftsmanship as a carpenter, mason, architect and painter and in this way he won the hearts of the native Indians. Here in this village he introduced the coffee tree which soon spread into many other cities and countries in South America. (Ban, DSB, Ham)

An extra glimpse of the early Society

One of many commemorative stamps celebrating Bartolomeu Gusmao's imaginative manned-flight experiment in Lisbon,1709

Bartolomeu de Gusmao
(Brazilian 1685-17240)

Bartolomeu Gusmao

Bartolomeu taught physics and mathematics and was convinced of the possibility and the desirability of manned flight. After studying the problem, theorizing and experimenting, he organized a public flight experiment in 1709 at the royal court in Lisbon. Using hot air under a kind of umbrella, he successfully flew down from a high tower. When, however, he tried to fly upward, he momentarily got off the ground but in doing so set fire to a part of the king's house. "Fortunately the king did not take it ill", an onlooker later wrote. (DSB, JLx)

John Hardouin
(French: 1646-1729)

John Hardouin

John was a linguist, historian, philosopher, and theologian. He edited the councils of the Church, thus producing one of the most dependable and scholarly works of the early eighteenth century. Although John was known as a very generous man and a prodigious worker, he was quite outspoken and eccentric, having proposed a number of original but bizarre opinions. It was said of him: "For 40 years he labored to ruin his reputation but without succeeding." (Ban, Ham, JLx, Som)

Maximilian Hell

(Hungarian: 1720-1792)

Maximilian Hell in Lapland

Maximilian taught mathematics in the Jesuit college at Leutschau, Hungary (now in Czechoslovakia). Later he was made director of the astronomy observatory in Vienna. After the Suppression of the Jesuits he continued working there as director, along with other members of the Society. Maximilian fell victim to the public defamation of Jesuits then in vogue when he was accused of altering his findings during a transit of Venus. His name was not cleared until a century later when in 1883 the famous astronomer Simon Newcomb found his readings to be correct, and his scholarship above suspicion. A 1970 Czechoslovakian stamp honors this Hungarian astronomer, dressed as a Laplander. It was in Lapland that he observed the transit of Venus across the sun's surface, the first one to do so.

Because of his many scientific adventures Maximilian was elected to the most prestigious scientific academies of Europe. For 37 years he published his unique periodical *Ephemerides Astronomicae*, containing the scientific treatises and important observations of European scientists. At this time Jesuits directed 30 of the world's 130 major astronomical observatories. Maximilian had been so successful in setting up smaller observatories that in 1755 Maria Theresa of Austria and Hungary named Maximilian her court astronomer and commissioned him to organize a great central observatory in Vienna.

Hell's other adventures included experiments in applying magnetism to medicine. This was uncharted ground, but by assuming unconventional premises Hell started something quite remarkable. Using lodestone he devised an arrangement of magnetic plates for the lessening of pain from illnesses such as rheumatism from which he himself suffered. He met with considerable success in relieving the pain. His magnetic medicine attracted the attention of a young man named Franz Mesmer, recently graduated from the Jesuit University of Dillingen in Bavaria. Mesmer disregarded the magnets and developed a different, but even more peculiar theory of healing based on circulating cosmic fluids in the body. Although the special hypotheses of both men were found to be groundless they had found a way to make suffering patients oblivious to pain. Eventually later investigators of these phenomena made "mesmerism", or hypnotism, an accepted medical practice. A lunar crater is named after Maximilian Hell. (Ban, DSB, Ham, JLx, Som)

Com. stamp of Hell's transit observation

An extra glimpse of the early Society

In his book, *Jesuit science in the age of Galileo,* William Ashworth describes the efforts made in the Jesuit colleges at collaboration with other scientists and the mutual support they provided for the sciences.

The Society of Jesus in the 17th century contained within its ranks an astonishing number of enthusiastic students of the natural world. Indeed, for the first sixty years of the century, the Jesuits were the only scientific society in existence anywhere. At a time when experimental science was decidedly unfashionable, Jesuits were charting sunspots, calibrating pendulums, timing the fall of weights off towers, and devising a variety of ingenious inventions. Indeed, in the fields of geometry, optics, magnetism, cartography, mechanics, and earth sciences, most of the principal authorities throughout the century were members of the Society of Jesus. The Jesuits were a remarkably bold and imaginative scientific body. (Ashworth, 1986, p.5)

Thomas Holland
(English: 1600-1642)

Thomas Holland

Thomas was one of the victims of the many priest-hunters in London who eagerly made their living by betraying priests for money. Thomas ministered to the beleaguered Catholics under very difficult conditions in cramped quarters. He carried on his ministry at night or in the early morning and had to stay indoors during the day, not even able to walk in the garden. Thomas became a master of disguises, using different aliases and passing himself off as a foreigner since he was fluent in French, Flemish, and Spanish. Finally he was arrested on suspicion of being a priest and was brought to Newgate prison for trial where he was found guilty and condemned to death. His response was "Thanks be to God" and a few days later he was hanged, drawn and quartered. (Ban, Bas, Ham, Tyl)

Sidronius de Hossche
(Belgian: 1596-1653)

Sidronius de Hossche

Sidronius was a Latin poet who wrote *The Tears of St. Peter,* a book of poems on the repentance and sorrow of Peter after his denial of Christ. He wrote *The Course of Human Life,* nine elegies, all of which use sea and ship imagery. Sidronius taught for a few years at the court of the Hapsburg prince, Archduke Leopold William of Austria, Governor of the Spanish Netherlands. But life at court did not suit this simple shepherd's son, and Sidronius turned to preaching. His poetic works were first printed as occasional pieces upon such events as the publication of some theological treatises by Leonard Lessius, S.J. or as an act of thanksgiving to the Blessed Virgin. (Ham, JLx, JLP)

An extra glimpse of the early Society

IHS

The seal of the Society contains the letters IHS referring to the first three Greek letters of the name JESUS after whom the Society is named.

iota, **I = J**   eta, **H = E**   and sigma **S = S**

(The Greek letter sigma for S has two forms Σ and **S**; more often the latter was used when the S came at the end of the word.) In Catholic tradition this symbol **IHS** was used for the name Jesus long before the Society of Jesus started.

Vincent   Huby
(French: 1608-1693)

Vincent   Huby

Vincent was a disciple of the renowned spiritual director Louis Lallemant during a period when some French Jesuits felt that the Society, with an exaggerated activity, had become too immersed in its apostolates to the detriment of their spiritual life. Lallemant's teaching is found in the book entitled *The Life and Spiritual Doctrine of Father Louis Lallemant.* Vincent Huby founded several retreat houses in Nantes, Quimper, Rennes and Vannes and is best remembered for his ability to organize the retreats and attract large numbers to make the Spiritual Exercises. (Ban, Ham, JLx, Som)

An extra glimpse of the early Society

There is no understanding Jesuits without some idea of Ignatius' *Spiritual Exercises . . .* unquestionably one of the most influential books ever written. It has been published some 4,500 times, an average of once a month for 400 years. The number of copies printed has been estimated to be some 4.5 million—despite the fact that the book is about as dry and uninspiring as a teacher's manual. For that is what the *Spiritual Exercises* are, a how-to handbook with a set of directions for directors on how to discern and decide amid the cacophony of conflicting voices, how to hear the voice of God who speaks in the deeper stillness of the heart; amid the many options regarding what to do with one's life, how to respond. (from *America*, 1995, **172**(3) by Ronald Modras)

Bl. William Ireland

(English: 1636-1679)

William   Ireland

William was an English martyr falsely accused in the 1678 plot of Titus Oates, a renegade Anglican minister, who out of hatred for the Jesuits concocted a bizarre story accusing the English Jesuits of planning the assassination of the king, of overthrowing government and of reinstating the Catholic Church. This fabricated "Popish" plot roused the fury of the nation and renewed Catholic persecutions. William Ireland, traveling under the name Ironmonger, was arrested along with others and thrown into the Newgate Prison where he suffered for three months before his trial. Titus Oates testified falsely that he had been present at the special conference of Jesuits planning the assassination, and it would have succeeded except for a faulty pistol. Although William could produce many witnesses to prove that he was in Wales at that time, it took only one bribed witness for William to be convicted of high treason and to be sentenced to be hanged, drawn, and quartered. The execution was postponed by royal order, because King Charles II never believed that the Jesuits were associated with any plot against him. Eventually, fearing the people's anger, Charles allowed the executions to take place in order to appease the crowd. At Tyburn William professed his innocence and denied any complicity against the king's life, then added; "I beg God Almighty to shower down a thousand blessings upon this whole kingdom." (Bas, Cor, Ham, JLx, Tyl)

St. Francis Jerome
(Italian: 1642-1716)

Francis Jerome

Francis had an apostolate among the poor slum-dwellers in Southern Italy, spending almost all his time with them in the most unsanitary and disreputable parts of the cities. He brought them the ministry of the Word, the sacraments of Penance and the Eucharist. He had entered the Jesuits already an ordained priest of 10 years and was sent into the streets of Naples. He would go about preaching and urging his hearers to come to Mass and Communion on the Communion Days, which at the time occurred only on the third Sunday of the month. He spent Monday and Saturday preaching in the streets of Naples and Tuesday to Friday preaching in the suburbs. It was said that he sometimes gave up to 40 short sermons in a single day. When the third Sunday arrived, no one was surprised to see that the Masses at the Church were crowded.

He would also visit the slaves who were chained to their places and would try to console and relieve their suffering in whatever way he could. When Francis requested to go to the Japanese missions, his Superior's response was: "the Kingdom of Naples is to be your Japan." Some clerics tried to obstruct his work by reporting to the Bishop that Francis who was occupied with street preaching and the worst kind of sinners was not suitable to give retreats to priests and nuns who were living in virtue. Restrictions were then put on Francis' work, but he continued his labors in Naples and its suburbs until 1702 when he was asked to carry his mission outside Naples to distant places. Eventually the entire Kingdom of Naples heard about his prophecies and his healings, and everyone considered him a distinguished preacher, not because his sermons possessed classical elegance, but because his simple language and expressions were filled with earnestness and conviction of the truth. (Ban, Cor, JLx, Som, Tyl)

St. Isaac Jogues

(French: 1607-1646)

Isaac Jogues

Isaac was martyred for the faith at Ossernenon in upstate New York. Born in Orleans, France, he entered the Jesuits at Rouen, studied philosophy at la Flèche slightly after René Descartes studied there. After ordination he came to Quebec in "New France" from where he was assigned to work with the Huron nation which num- bered around 30,000. This meant a canoe trek of over 800 miles, which included carry- ing the canoe overland past cascades. The mission there, called "Sainte Marie," was b y then a thriving enterprise. Jesuits had taught the natives how to cultivate the land and care for cattle and fowl. Other tribes, such as the Chippewas, were so impressed that they asked the Jesuits to start a mission among their people. In 1642, Isaac was captured by the Mohawks, one o f the five Iroquois nations, and taken to Auriesville in New York State. During his 13-month captivity he was subject to brutal cruelties. Nevertheless he taught Christianity to those who would listen and succeeded in baptizing 60 members of the tribe. Eventually he was rescued by the Dutch of Fort Orange and returned to France in 1644. While recuperating in France and preparing to return to his mission among the Mohawks, who had treated him so dreadfully four years earlier, he wrote to a fellow Jesuit: "My heart tells me that if I have the blessing of being sent on this mission, I shall not return." That year when h e returned to New France, he was tomahawked to death while on a peace mission to the Iroquois. (Ban, Cor, Ham, JLx, Som, Tyl)

Joseph   Jouvancy
(French: 1643-1719)

Joseph   Jouvancy

Joseph   was   one   of   France's   most distinguished   teachers.   In   his *History of the Society of Jesus,* h e narrated   the story   of the   Society's expulsion   from   France   in   1594 and the   condemnation   by Parlia- ment   of Bellarmine,   Suarez,   and Santarelli.   This accusations   stung the   French   Parliament   who took their   revenge   on   the   Society   re- sulting   in   a great   deal   of   political problems   for   the   French   Jesuits.

Joseph   felt   strongly   that   the only   those   expert   in   Latin   and Greek   were   truly   educated,   a view   not   shared   by many.   One of his   companions   retorted: "Hardly   ten   out   of   a thousand alumni,   even   with   a full   course   in   the   humanities   and philosophy,   could   write   a good   letter.   The   Latin   and composition   work   given   them   is so   monotonous   that   it inevitably   leads   to   idleness   and   boredom."   Later   Jesuits sought   a freer   and   wider   curriculum   maintaining   that: "The   concept   of humanism   is not   itself   identified   with   a n y specific   category   of subjects   as such."   Regarding   Jesuit school   dramatic   presentations,   Joseph   also   fought   another losing   battle   opposing   comedy   in   school   plays   because "this   form   of art   easily   leads   to   all   kinds   of   buffoonery, which   is not   compatible   with   the   religious   training   of t h e young."   (Ban, Ham, JLx, Som)

Francis   Kareu
(Lithuanian: 1731-1802)

Francis   Kareu

Francis was appointed Superior General for the Jesuits in Russia, during the time of the Suppression (1773-1814) and recognized by Pope Pius VII as "duly charged and entrusted with the requisite and necessary authority to follow and maintain the rule of St. Ignatius Loyola." When Pope Clement IV's papal nuncio tried to persuade Tsaritsa Catherine to promulgate the brief of the Suppression of the Society, *Dominus ac Redemptor,* Catherine replied that she regarded it as her most important duty to promote national education and was, therefore, unable to despoil an order which devoted itself so zealously to educational work. At the age of 64 Francis was elected Vicar general and in 1801 Pope Pius VII directed that Francis Kareu and his successors be known as Superior General of the Society, and no longer merely Vicar-general. (Ban, Ham, JLx, Som)

Leonard   Kessel
(Belgian: 1518-1574)

**Ignatius Loyola appearing
to Leonard Kessel**

Leonard was the first rector of the College for Jesuit "scholastics" (not yet ordained) in Cologne. He was told by Peter Canisius that the principal reason for the years of study enjoined upon Jesuit scholastics was to make them effective preachers. Leonard also reported that Ignatius prescribed that no academic discipline that could help preachers was to be neglected. Leonard also encouraged opening to non-Jesuit students these schools which were originally meant only for Jesuits. He sent Ignatius his opinion that if Jesuits would begin to teach publicly, there is every hope for "gaining all youth to Christ". About this time Ignatius was doing just that, opening schools in Gandia, Messina, and Palermo. By 1551, because of financial support by the duke of Gandia the Collegio Romano in Rome opened for non-Jesuit students and over its door hung the inscription "School of Grammar, Humanities, and Christian Doctrine, Free". (Ban, Ham, O'M)

Peter Kasui Kibé
(Japanese: 1587-1639)

Peter, an educated descendent
of Japanese sailors, was exiled
to Macao by a Shogun. Then h e
traversed Persia en route to
Jerusalem, then to Rome to b e
ordained. He returned to t h e
Orient and spent several y e a r s
in clandestine ministry to
Christian fugitives along t h e
Mekong River (today's
Thailand). He finally r e a c h e d
Japan and worked u n -
derground until his capture.

Peter Kasui Kibé

He was then tortured and hung over the infamous "sulfur
pits" until he died. (JLx)

An extra glimpse of the early Society

Jesuit artists in China included men such as Brossard, Sickelpart, Panzi,
Sallusti, Poirot and Castiglione. The Chinese would have sacrificed all their
possessions for the opportunities these Jesuit artists had to speak with the
emperor. Since the emperor visited the Jesuit art studios, Jesuits had a special
opportunity to seek his mercy on behalf of the persecuted Chinese Christians.
For instance when Emperor K'ien-lung expressed his satisfaction with one of his
frescos Brother Castiglione took the occasion to beg mercy for a group of
tormented Chinese Christians. K'ien-lung told him to be calm and continue his
painting. Then he ordered his ministers to cease the persecution.

Bl. Leonard Kimura

(Japanese: 1575-1619)

Leonard Kimura

Leonard Kimura was one of the 33 Jesuits who died during the Great Persecution. His grandfather was the first Japanese person to be baptized by Francis Xavier. His family lived in Nagasaki and there he attended the Jesuit school and for a dozen or so years served as lay catechist traveling with the Jesuit priests on their missionary trips. Leonard became a Jesuit Coadjutor Brother, served as cook and tailor and again took up his catechetical career and joined the fathers on their apostolic journeys. When the Jesuits were expelled in 1614 Leonard stayed behind and for several years worked alone and lived the life of a fugitive. Eventually he was captured with a small group of Christians. At the time of his arrest he was dressed as a Japanese gentleman and his captors did not know that they had caught a Jesuit in their net. At his trial the judge offered him the usual 200 pieces of silver if he would reveal the whereabouts of a Jesuit priest, but Br. Kimura honestly answered, "I know one Jesuit; he is a Coadjutor Brother and not a priest and I am that Brother."

Because of this admission he was sent to prison. There he did catechetical work and set about instructing the jailers and non-Christian prisoners in the fundamentals of the Catholic faith. Over this long period he made 96 converts and transformed the prison into a Christian community with fixed times for prayer and meditation. At his trial Governor Gonroku condemned him to "death by slow fire." A contemporary who attended the execution of Leonard and his four companions recorded that there were about 20,000 people present. Never did they see five men die so joyfully. (Ban, Cor, Tyl)

S.G. Eusebio Kino
(Italian: 1645-1711)

Eusebio Kino

Eusebio was born in the Italian Alps not far from Trent. He entered the Jesuits and after his training was assigned to the Indies. He was pleased with this assignment since his patron was St. Francis Xavier. Later, however, his assignment was changed, sending him to America. He had been a teacher of mathematics, but besides this skill he also brought with him a thorough training in astronomy, geography and cartography. Then in the New World he became a colonizer, a cattleman, an agriculturist, a builder and an historian of the development of the West. He arrived in Mexico in 1681. The Indians loved and respected him, and soon he became for the Pima Indians their friend, their father, their protector and their educator. Eusebio founded 24 missions, 19 ranches and a number of towns; he explored and mapped Sonora and Southern Arizona and proved that Lower California was not an island, as had been widely believed, but a peninsula. Indefatigable rider, he seemed to live in the saddle. He taught the Indians how to raise cattle. After 30 years of very productive work, he died while celebrating High Mass at the dedication of a new Church in honor of Francis Xavier in Magdalena. The town changed its name to Magdalena de Kino.

Besides being a dedicated and enthusiastic missionary Kino was the first real scientific explorer of the vast American Southwest, one of its great cartographers and explorers. Mexico has a commemorative stamp so to honor him. The National Statuary Hall in Washington, D.C., inaugurated in 1864, celebrated its 100th anniversary by inducting Eusebio Kino into its "Hall of Fame" in 1964 . Each of the 50 states has two representatives in Statuary Hall. Eusebio was the choice of the State of Arizona, thus making him the second Jesuit after Père Marquette to be so honored. Arizona also honors him with a large equestrian statue in the middle of the bustling city of Tucson. (Ban, DSB, JLx, Som, Tyl)

Athanasius Kircher

(German: 1602-1680)

Athanasius Kircher

Athanasius taught at the Roman College for many years and wrote on numerous scientific subjects. With contributions to almost every branch of science such as mathematics, astronomy, harmonics, acoustics, chemistry, microscopy and medicine, he played a significant part in the early scientific revolution. He was also a phenomenal linguist, an avid collector of scientific experiments and of geographical exploration. He probed the secrets of the subterranean world, deciphered archaic languages, experimented with music-therapy, optics and magnetism. In his 39 books on the sciences, some quite massive, he shows his learning of the past, ever open to the developments and possibilities of the future. His *Kircher Museum* was considered one of the best science museums in the world. Among his inventions are listed the megaphone, the pantometrum for solving geometrical problems, and a counting machine. His discoveries include sea phosphorescence as well as microscopically small organisms (germs) which transmit epidemic diseases. It was by facilitating a wide diffusion of knowledge, by stimulating thought and discussion by his vast collections of scientific information, that Kircher earned a place among the fathers of modern science and the titles of *"universal genius"* and *"master of a hundred arts"*. (Ban, DSB, Ham, JLx, Som)

St. James Kisai
(Japanese: 1533-1597)

James and companions

James was born of a pagan family and raised a Buddhist, but he was later baptized. He married a Christian and she bore him a son. His wife eventually decided to return to her former Buddhist beliefs. When he was unable to talk her out of her decision, he separated from her and entrusted his son to a Christian family in order to insure the child's proper upbringing. James then went to Osaka and found employment with the Jesuits working around the house and caring for the guests. When the Jesuits saw how well he knew and lived his Faith, they made him a catechist and eventually he became a novice Coadjutor Brother. He was arrested with Paul Miki, taken to a prison and with 22 others condemned to be crucified in Nagasaki. As the 24 prisoners were led to a hill for execution, two Christians tried to comfort them and they were added to those who were to die. All 26 were crucified. (Ban, JLx, Tan)

26 Martyrs Shrine in Nagasaki

St. Stanislaus Kostka
(Polish: 1550-1568)

Stanislaus   Kostka

Stanislaus, as a 17 year-old student at the Jesuit College i n Vienna, gave the measure of his determination to respond to God's call to the Jesuit Society,   against   the   set opposition of his angered father and a sadistic brother, by the fatiguing journeys h e made on foot from Vienna to Augsburg, and then on to t h e Jesuit novitiate in Rome.

In 1567 the Roman Noviti-ate of Saint Andrea was started, and one year later, this 1 8-year-old   novice   died. Stanislaus   was   recognized   f o r accomplishing the ordinary things in life in an extraordi-nary way through a vibrant faith. The liturgy speaks of him "accomplishing   much in a short time". Saints h a v e always   fascinated   ordinary   people   like   ourselves:'. t h e y matter   a   great   deal.   John   Coleman   says   that   personal holiness "shatters   our   ordinary   notions   of what   makes human   life   whole.   Saints   disrupt   conventional assumptions about what is real and worth our while a n d what is not." It is not often that a brand new religious n o-vitiate is blessed by the presence of a saint among its first novices. (Ban, Cor, Ham, JLx, Som, Tyl)

An extra glimpse of the early Society

In 1658 the great Giovanni Lorenzo Bernini began working on the new Jesuit Novitiate church of Sant' Andrea al Quirinale in Rome. Eventually Bernini created one of the most handsome baroque churches in Rome. To Bernini Sant' Andrea brought a personal satisfaction he did not derive from any of his other works, and there he went when he sought interior peace and consolation.

Claude   Lacroix
(French: 1652-1714)

Claude   Lacroix

Claude taught moral theology at Munster and Co-
logne. His great 1714 work
Theologia moralis became
one of the outstanding
theological works of the
18th century. Unfortu-
nately, Claude found him-
self embroiled in disputes
which concerned the
numbers of gold pieces
needed to constitute the
"grave sum" in a theft, the
number of grams of food
that might be eaten on
fast-days, the number of days a banned book can be kept
and how many pages of such a book may be read. He is used
as an example of the similarity between Jesuit moral
theology and the prescriptions of the Jewish *Mishnah* in
the Talmud. When someone was trying to illustrate that the
Jesuits and the Jews are alike in spirit, Jesuits were
charged with having perverted the clear moral laws of the
Gospel into "subtle Talmudic formulas". Nevertheless
Theologia moralis went through 25 editions in only half a
century and won for Claude the reputation of being one of
the finest moralists of his age. One of the later editions
served as a focal point of the opposition of the Jansenists to
the Jesuits and was condemned by the parliament of Paris
and publicly burned at Toulouse. (Ham, JLx, Som)

Joseph Lafiteau
(French: 1681-1746)

Joseph Lafiteau

Joseph was a *Visitor* to the Jesuit mission in Canada after having served a term as mission director in Rome. He has been called "The Father of Cultural Anthropology" because of his 1724 book *Customs of the American Indians* which displayed keen observation and understanding gained through many years of study of the Iroquois culture, language and habits. Joseph as well as other French Jesuits of the time followed the practice started by the Spanish and German Jesuit missionaries in Arizona and California of publishing their reflections concerning Native American life. (Ban, Ham, JLx, Som)

An extra glimpse of the early Society

In his *Italian Journey* Johann Wolfgang von Goethe expressed his admiration for "the Jesuit churches which secretly inspired all people with reverence". In this vein he also wrote also about Jesuit drama.

This public performance has again convinced me of the cleverness of the Jesuits. They despised nothing which could in any way be effective. There are some (Jesuits) who devote themselves with knowledge and inclination to the theater in the same manner in which they distinguish their churches by a pleasing magnificence. These intelligent men here have made themselves masters of the worldly senses by means of a theater worthy of respect.

William Lamormaini

(Luxembourg: 1570-1648)

William   Lamormaini

William was confessor to Ferdinand II, Emperor of Austria, for the duration of the Thirty Years' War, prompting the papal nuncio at Vienna to report: "It is certain that the Jesuits, through the favor of the emperor, which cannot be overestimated, have attained to overwhelming power. They have the upper hand over everything . . . . Their influence has always been considerable, but it has reached its zenith since Father Lamormaini has been confessor to the emperor." In I629, another Jesuit confessor to France's Louis XIII, John Suffren, together with William Lamormaini tried to prevent France entering this War. Both thought they had succeeded, having convinced their respective rulers, but both had miscalculated the growing influence of Cardinal Richelieu who had seized control of the policy of France. He fired John Suffren and convinced the weak king not to make peace with Ferdinand but to enter the war against Austria and Spain. William Lamormaini won a later victory, however, by convincing Ferdinand II to undo past injustices against the Church by restoring the bishoprics, parishes, and monasteries taken by the Protestants. (Ban, Ham, JLx, Som)

Raphael   Landivar
(Spanish: 1731-1793)

Raphael   Landivar

Raphael worked as a mission-ary to Latin America and is called "Guatemala's greatest poet". Even the taxi drivers can quote "The all-time poet laureate of Guatemala". The 15 books of his epic *Rusticatio Mexicana* are composed of 5,000 lines of Latin hexame-ters. He describes the Indian pastimes of handball, greased pole, cockfights and bull fights and he exhorts youth to appreciate nature's beautiful gifts. Originally buried in Bologna, his body was moved when Guatemala students petitioned their government to bring the remains of Guatemala's illustrious son home. The University in Guatemala is named *Landivar* in his honor. (JLx, Som)

An extra glimpse of the early Society

The Jesuit Paraguay Reductions started in 1610 (57 Settlements serving 113,716 Native Americans) and ended in 1767. The historian, Arnold Toynbee, summed up the creation and destruction of this noble enterprise. "A summer of unwonted peace and prosperity terminated by the Spanish crown's wanton crime of liquidating an idyllic hierocracy."

Diego　Laynez
(Spanish: 1512-1565)

Diego came from a wealthy family of Castile, now considered "New Christians" because his great-grandfather had converted from Judaism to Christianity. This fearless and intelligent man, Diego, became one of the first seven companions of Ignatius Loyola. He spent his life preaching and teaching in Italy, became Jesuit provincial in Italy and later the second Superior General of the Jesuits. Diego was one of the great men of the Catholic reform and, at his death, Pius V said that the Church had lost one of its best

Diego Laynez

experts. During the Council of Trent he served as papal theologian and as a Council father and his five addresses to the Council were considered masterpieces of learning and clarity. He argued quite energetically against Spanish Bishops who opposed papal power over the episcopacy. As Superior General of the Jesuits he assisted the pope in carrying out the reforms of the Council. He had important contributions to make on subjects as diverse as justification, the certitude of the *state of grace*, penance and purgatory, an *Index of Errors* about the Sacraments, the Real Presence, penances and the Sacrifice of the Mass, Communion under both species for the laity, Holy Orders, annulment of clandestine marriages and the jurisdiction of bishops. At a fourth centenary celebration of the Council of Trent, Diego was considered one of the leading figures in the council's work. (Ban, Ham, JLx, O'M, Som)

Antonio   Lecchi
(Italian: 1702-1776)

Antonio   Lecchi

Antonio was a physicist and specialized in hydrostatics. Maria Theresa chose Antonio as her court mathematician and Pope Clement XIII made him director of hydraulics. When Clement XIV, who suppressed the Society, arrived on the scene, however, Antonio resigned from this position. Cardinal Albani regretted his departure and wrote a very flattering account of Antonio's scientific contributions to the Church in the *Florence Gazette*. (Ban, Ham, JLx, Som)

An extra glimpse of the early Society

In his book *God and Nature,* David Lindberg describes the early collaborative efforts of Jesuits.

Another admirable feature of the Jesuit scientific enterprise was their appreciation of the value of collaboration. One might well argue that the *Society of Jesus,* rather than the *Accademia del Cimento* or the *Royal Society*, was the first true scientific society. [The Jesuit] Kircher, the impressario of Rome, was more than a match for Mersenne and Boulliau in Paris or Henry Oldenburg in London, in his ability to collect observations and objects from a worldwide network of informants. More important, Kircher published this information in massive encyclopedias, which together with similar efforts from Schott and Riccioli, were as vital as the early scientific journals in disseminating scientific information. If scientific collaboration was one of the outgrowths of the scientific revolution, the Jesuits deserve a large share of the credit. (Lindberg, p.155)

James   Ledesma
(Spanish: 1519-1575)

James Ledesma

Before he entered the Society James taught philosophy
and theology at some of the
more celebrated universities
of Europe: Salamanca, Paris
and Louvain. He had studied
at the universities of Alcalá,
Paris, and Louvain and became one of the important
architects of the educational
program for the Jesuit
schools. James published in
Italy a catechism for the
"very ignorant" and another
for the "less ignorant." The
general structure of
catechisms were influenced by the catechism of Peter
Canisius. James' work ran through many editions and
translations well into the seventeenth century and were
even used with the indigenous peoples in New France.
(Ban, Ham, JLx, O'M, Som)

Simon LeMoyne
(French: 1604-1697)

Simon LeMoyne

Simon entered the Jesuit Novitiate at Rouen and later
became an instructor there.
After his ordination Simon
was assigned to the Canadian
Mission, arriving in the City
of Quebec in 1638. He then
went to the Huron country
where, in the company of
Brebeuf, Jogues, Daniel and
Lalemant he quickly mas-
tered the Huron, Iroquois
and Algonquin languages -
better, it is reported, than
any of the 300 Jesuits who
were to work in the New
France mission from 1611 to 1800. He lived through the
horror of the destruction of the Huron mission, after
which he moved to Quebec.

Since the Iroquois were threatening the existence of
New France, the French governor sent Simon as an
ambassador of peace to the Iroquois and Onondaga in 1654.
He made his tedious month-long journey by canoe which,
when overturned on land, provided his only shelter from
the rain and snow. He came across some of the Christian
Hurons who were then captives of the Iroquois and also
met Iroquois that he had befriended in the past. He was
able to administer the sacraments to many along the way.
Finally he arrived at the place of the council with the
Iroquois at an Onondaga village, near what is now
Syracuse.

Simon was called *Ondessonk* (Eagle) by the Indians. He
related his adventures in letters to France which were
preserved in *The Jesuit Relations* (XVI #102-125). "At each
of my presentations, they uttered a loud shout of applause
from the depths of their chest, in evidence of their delight.
I was occupied fully two hours in delivering my entire
harangue, which I pronounced in the tone of a Captain -
walking back and forth, as is their custom, like an actor on
a stage." As a result of his moving presentation Simon was

given the seat of honor and rejoicing started as soon as the
Council declared their decision to accept his arguments
and commit themselves to four propositions: that they
would acknowledge the governor of New France as their
master, that all assemblies and peace parleys would be held
at Onondaga Village; that a site be chosen by the French
for a settlement in their Onondaga country and finally that
the French and Iroquois would henceforth live at peace
with one another.

After this four-day meeting Simon set out for Quebec.
He was given a few relics of his companions on the Huron
mission: the New Testament of John de Brebeuf, S.J. and a
small devotional work that had belonged to Charles
Garnier, S.J., both of whom had been martyred by the
Iroquois four years before. Simon's last recorded act of his
ministry among the Onondagas on this visit occurred on
August 15th when he baptized his first Onondaga convert,
to whom he gave the name of John the Baptist, a zealous
young captain, "chief of eighteen hundred men."

Then Simon related his experience on the shore of
Onondaga Lake. "We arrived at the entrance to a little lake
in a great basin that is half dried up, and taste the water
from a spring of which these people dare not drink as they
say there is an evil spirit in it that renders it foul. Upon
tasting of it, I find it to be a spring of salt water; and indeed
we made some salt from it, as natural as that which comes
from the sea, and are carrying a sample of it to Quebec.
This lake is very rich in salmon, trout and other fish." This
is the first reference in history to the salt springs of
Onondaga, which later became so well known and which
contributed more than any other single factor to the
growth and prosperity of the once twin villages of Salina
and Syracuse.

Back in Quebec, Simon's report was favorably received
and he made four subsequent journeys to the Iroquois
country on missions of peace to the hostile Mohawks. He
can properly be called the precursor of the Onondaga
mission. He was more than ordinarily proficient in the
Huron-Iroquois dialects, as well as in the subtleties of
Indian oratory and diplomacy. His writings in the form of
diaries, letters and reports as found in the *Jesuit Relations*
have preserved a simple and moving history of Central
New York of those days. In 1946 the New York Jesuit
Province founded a school in Syracuse and named
LeMoyne College to honor Simon LeMoyne. (Ban, JLx, Som)

Leonard Lessius
(Flemish: 1554-1623)

Leonard Lessius

Leonard taught at the English College of Douai (Belgium) and at Louvain. He studied under the great Spanish Jesuit theologian Francisco de Suarez. At Louvain he quickly established a reputation for outstanding intellectual ability and was hailed as 'Prince of Philosophers' and 'Oracle of the Low Countries'. Lessius figured prominently in the controversies then raging on the nature of grace, adopting a position closely akin to that of the Spanish Jesuit Luis de Molina; in 1610 he published his principal work on this subject, *De gratia efficaci*. Lessius launched an attack on the divine right of kings as proposed by James I of England. In 1613 Suarez's writings on this subject were publicly burnt in London by royal command. But Lessius's most important book was *De justitia et jure* (1605), which was published throughout Europe in some forty separate editions. This work was notable especially for its analysis of contemporary commercial practice; Lessius' opinions on the morality of various business arrangements exercised a substantial influence on the thinking of statesmen and church leaders. King Albert the Pius always kept Lessius's book on justice on the table before him as his most trusted counselor when he held hearings, to show that his decisions were buttressed "by the arms of Austria and the wisdom of Lessius". Lessius made major contributions to the development of economic analysis. (Ban, Ham, JLx, Som)

David Lewis
(English: 1617-1679)

David Lewis

David was a victim of the so-called Titus Oates plot. Titus was twice expelled from European Jesuit schools and was later refused admission into the Society, so he spread the story that the Jesuits were plotting to overthrow England's king and make the country Catholic once again, thereby depriving many landowners of the estates confiscated from Catholic lands. After David's arrest, one of his examiners was Titus Oates who was unable to make any charge stick, but David was condemned anyway. He then gave such a moving speech at the gallows that it was later published. "I believe you are here met not only to see a fellow-native die, but also with expectation to hear a dying fellow native speak. I suffer not as a murderer, thief, or such like malefactor, but as a Christian, and therefore am not ashamed. My religion is the Roman Catholic; in it I have lived above these 40 years; in it I now die, and so fixedly die, that if all the good things in this world were offered me to renounce, all should not move me one hair's breath from my Roman Catholic faith. A Roman Catholic I am; a Roman Catholic priest I am; a Roman Catholic priest of that religious order called the Society of Jesus I am, and I bless God who first called me." The hangman fled the scene, fearing the crowd would stone him but the job was finished by a man bribed to take the executioner's place. (Ban, Bas, Ham, Tyl)

Claude   Linyères
(French: 1658-1746)

Claude taught mathematics at the college of La Flèche. He also directed many in the spiritual exercises of St. Ignatius, was superior of a retreat house and gave spiritual direction. He served as spiritual advisor for the Duchess of Orleans for four years and for King Louis XV for 26 years. (Ham)

Claude   Linyères

St.   Ignatius Loyola
(Basque: 1490-1556)

Ignatius is the founder of the Society of Jesus, the author of the *Spiritual Exercises*, and the Patron Saint of all Jesuits. Over his own protests he was elected the first Superior General. The expansion of the Jesuit Society was nothing less than miraculous; during his 16 years as Superior General it had grown from 10 men to 1,000 men living in 101 houses. Ignatius was canonized in 1622.

Ignatius   Loyola

Iñigo de Oñaz y Loyola was born in the Basque hill country, the youngest of 11 children. Having received only a superficial education, he was mainly interested in sports and military prowess. While defending a fort in

Pamplona, his leg was broken. During his convalescence he underwent a remarkable conversion and was determined to imitate the saints and to become a knight in the service of God. After some years in prayer and penance in Manresa, near Barcelona, he received divine illumination by which the rest of his life would be guided. He wrote down his experiences in his famous book known as the *Spiritual Exercises*. These *Exercises* are not meant to be merely read - they are meant to be put into practice. They involve a process meant to free one to choose what is best for oneself in the light of first principles, and to bring a sense that God is at work in all things, animating and energizing them. These step-by-step guidelines for teaching the art of prayer and meditation are divided into four parts considering the sinful nature of mankind, the Incarnation of Christ, the Passion and, finally, the Resurrection. They are meant to lead an individual to find God in all things, to increase awareness of God's plan and the role one can play in this life.

In both Alcalá and Salamanca Ignatius was reported to the Spanish Inquisition and jailed. Later in Paris he gathered together six companions who determined to go to Rome and put themselves at the disposal of the pope who exclaimed on seeing them: "The finger of God is here." In

1540 Pope Paul III gave formal recognition to the Order which would profess the three customary vows of poverty, chastity and obedience along with a fourth vow of special obedience to the pope. The name *Loyola* is engraved on the walls of educational institutions throughout the world such as the Sorbonne in Paris and Columbia University in New York. (Ban, Cor, Ham, JLx, O'M, Som, Tyl)

Ignatius inspired to write down the SPIRITUAL EXERCISES

John de Lugo
(Spanish: 1583-1660)

John was a brilliant theologian who brought to the lecture halls of Valladolid ele-
gant expression, clear expo-
sitions and profound doc-
trine. John taught at the Roman College from 1621-643
and then was made a cardinal. This appointment did not
please him since he had to
leave his theological re-
search which come to us in
his books. One such was *Justice and Law* which was
highly lauded by St. Alphon-

John de Lugo

sus Liguori because of its lucid reasoning and accurate
judgment. This work had a great influence on other
theologians. John published little of the vast amount of
material he had prepared because he was a perfectionist,
polishing his works constantly. (Ban, Ham, JLx, Som)

Gabriel Malagrida
(Italian: 1689-1761)

Gabriel Malagrida

Gabriel popularized the retreat movement in Portugal after having worked for thirty years in Brazil. This very popular septuagenarian became a victim of the Marquis de Pombal's machinations to suppress the Society in Portugal. Pombal's plan was to involve Jesuits in whatever scandal he could invent and his opportunity came one evening when Portugal's King Joseph secretly visited the Marchioness of Tavora. He was shot at by the jealous husband who was merely trying to discourage these trysts. Pombal had the whole Tavora family imprisoned along with their confessor Gabriel Malagrida, and tried to convince fellow Portuguese that it was a Jesuit plot to kill the king. "Who had ever heard of the husband of a king's mistress making difficulties for the king, especially resorting to force?" Pombal insisted that the violent action of the young Tavora nobleman was such an astonishing reaction that he must have been instigated to shoot the king by these crafty and audacious Jesuits. The charge was soon dropped, but Pombal would not give up and had Gabriel Malagrida imprisoned and tried for heresy because of his past writings. Gabriel was tried by the Inquisition, anxious to punish heretics of any kind. He was not the first Jesuit to be tormented by this tribunal. Bagbriel was found guilty and was later burned at the stake. If it were not for the cowardice of Portugal's King Joseph the Marquis de Pombal would not have had this gruesome triumph over the Jesuits. Upon hearing of this crime Voltaire wrote: "Extreme embarrassment and absurdity have resulted in extreme horror." (Ban, Ham, JLx, Som)

John de Maldonado
Spanish: 1534-1583)

John de Maldonado

John created a sensation when he lectured on philosophy and theology at the College of Clermont in Paris. His brilliant exposition and broad erudition brought to life the traditionally boring courses in humane letters and philosophy, so that crowds of excited students filled his classroom. Sometimes he had more than 1,000 students in attendence and some even arrived two or three hours before the lecture to get a seat. John had broken with the older methods of commentary and showed how theology, studied in the documents of Scripture and patristic writings, was the best way to meet the present intellectual challenges. Embarrassed by the numbers of students following Jesuits like John Maldonado the university lecturers started a relentless campaign to dislodge this threatening Jesuit College of Clermont. They succeeded in getting rid of the troublesome John Maldonado by using Pope Gregory XIII who was worried about the turmoil at Paris. John was moved to the Sorbonne and then in Potiers, Bourges, Pont-à-Mousson and Bordeaux. (Ban, Ham, JLx, O'M, Som)

Ven. Jules Mancinelli

(Italian: 1558-1618)

Jules Mancinelli

Jules followed in the long lively Jesuit tradition of popular preaching begun by Ignatius and the earliest companions. Jules brought the force of his energetic personality far beyond Italy by a strenuous campaign in de-Christianized Dalmatia as well as to Constantinople where he gave renewed vigor to the Latin Catholics there. He also aroused interest in reunion with Rome among the Orthodox, and brought comfort to the Christian slaves in Turkey. (Ban, Ham, JLx, Som)

Juan   Mariana
(Spanish: 1537-1624)

Juan   Mariana

Juan   was   a   prodigious   Castilian   scholar   who   wrote   on   a
wide   variety   of   subjects.   He is
most   remembered   for   his   1599
book   *The   King   and   his
Formation*   which   recalls   a n
unfortunate   page   of   Jesuit
history.   One   of   his   topics   was
the   morality   of   tyrannicide.
He   supported   the   proposition
that   a   tyrant   should   be   removed   from   office,   killed   if
necessary,   except   by   poisoning,   once   the   people   had   made
the   decision   to   do   so.   This   was
quickly   and   solemnly   con-
demned   by   the   Superior   General   Aquaviva   and   later   by   a
General   Congregation   of   the   whole   Society   of   Jesus.
Careless   historians   have   neglected   to   point   out   this   Jesuit
condemnation   of   Juan's   ideas.   Spaniards   paid   little
attention   to   Juan's   thesis,   but   it   caused   a   great   stir   i n
France   partly   because   of   the   assassination   of   Henry   IV. A
century   later   John's   name   occasioned   the   now-familiar
image   of   Marianne   found   on   many   French   stamps.   This
was   meant   to   be   a   play   on   John   Mariana's   name,   and   was
used   as   the   symbol   of   the   French   Revolution.   The   French
extremists   used   John   Mariana's   thesis   to   justify   the
excesses   of   the   French   Revolution.   (Ban,   Ham,   JLx,   O'M,
Som)

Jacques Marquette
(French: 1637-1675)

Jacques Marquette

Born in Laon, France Jacques was one of the earliest Europeans to encounter the Native American Indians. He spoke six Amerindian languages, and only once did he encounter hostile Indians, but even then, it was not long before he was smoking a peace pipe with them. Jacques worked with the Illinois, the Pottawatamis, the Foxes, the Huron, the Ottawa and Sioux. When forced out by hostile Sioux he founded a new mission among the Mackinac which later became the Mission of St. Ignace. The Indians liked *Black Robes* such as Jacques: "They slept on the ground, exposed themselves to all privations and did not ask for money." Primarily a missionary, Jacques was most noted for his explorations, not the least of which was tracing the Mississippi and finding that it flowed not into the Atlantic, as was presumed, but into the Gulf of Mexico. For his invaluable explorations and his astonishing work with the Native American Indians he is celebrated with a heroic statue in Laon. Wisconsin chose to honor Jacques as

one of their two rep-resentatives in Stat-uary Hall in the Capital in Washing-ton, D. C. James was only 38 when he died.

(Ban, DSB, JLx, Som)

Marquette commemorative stamp

Marcel   Mastrilli
(Italian: 1603-1637)

Marcel & Xavier's picture

Marcel was a martyr during the virulent anti-Catholic persecution in Japan in 1637 during which 13 percent of the Catholic population of 300,000 were martyred. For two days Marcel set the endurance record for the *water torture*, having water continually poured into his mouth so that only by frantic efforts could he breathe. Marcel had had a premonition of this martyrdom from Francis Xavier four years previous while in a coma resulting from an accident. During renovations of a church in Naples a falling hammer struck him on the head. For several days he lingered at the point of death and doctors had abandoned any hope of his recovery. Francis Xavier appeared to him, reminded him of an earlier vow Marcel had made to go to the missions and also promised that all who prayed to Francis during nine successive days would experience the effects of Francis' intercession. Marcel awoke completely cured and later became famous for his propagation of devotion to St. Francis Xavier which is held every March from 3/4 to 3/12. In 1635 during his stop in Lisbon while on his way to the Indies, Marcel preached a series of nine sermons on St. Francis Xavier at the Jesuit church of St. Roque and by doing so had launched the very first *Novena of Grace*. (Ban, Ham, JLx, Som)

Bl. Julien Maunoir

(French: 1606-1683)

Julien Maunoir

Julien was a home missionary in Brittany for 43 years, even though he had requested to go to Canada with his classmate Isaac Jogues. Having learned the Breton language while teaching as a scholastic in Quimper, he was found to be uniquely suited for this difficult task of evangelizing the impoverished people of Brittany. Julien became the principal cause of religious renewal there. His missions bore great fruit sometimes attracting 10,000 to 30,000 individuals. On these occasions he usually asked the parish priests, whose parishioners were attending the mission, to help in hearing confessions, catechizing, and distributing the Eucharist. When these priests saw the good that was being derived from these missions, seven of them asked their bishop's permission to join Julien in his work. A grateful Julian immediately began training these assistants, called *Breton Missionaries*. He started in 1651 with seven, but by 1665 there were 300, and by 1683 almost 1000. (Ban, Cor, Ham, JLx, Som, Tyl)

Balthasar Mendez de Loyola

(Moroccan: 1531-1567)

Balthasar Mendez de Loyola

Balthasar was the son of the Sultan of Fez in Morocco and was raised a Muslim. Married at the age of 15 he soon became the parent of three children, but during a pilgrimage to Mecca, he was captured by a Christian garrison. Five years later he experienced a deep desire to become baptized, and in 1556 the year of Ignatius' death, he took the occasion of his baptism to change his last name from Mohammed Attaz to Mendez de Loyola. Later he joined the Society and went to work with Muslim slaves in Naples and Rome. (Ham, Jlx)

Claude
Ménestrier
(French: 1631-1705)

Claude was a teacher of literature at the Jesuit schools in Chambéry, Grenoble, Vienne, and Lyon. The French Jesuits meticulously developed drama in their schools as Jesuits in other countries were doing. They placed special emphasis on ballet which had become so important in

Claude   Ménestrier

France. In 1682 Claude published his important work *Ancient and Modern Ballets.* There was great variety in the ballets, some allegorical, some historical, some honored an important public event or person. Claude's plays were known for their elaborate stage settings. (Ban, Ham, JLx, Som)

Everard Mercurian

(Luxembourg: 1514-1580)

Everard   Mercurian

Everard was the fourth Superior General of the Society. He brought to the office a great deal of administrative experience as provincial, assistant, and visitor in Germany and France. In 1577 he issued rules and job descriptions for some of the important offices in the Society. Everard also attempted to systematize the Society's apostolic works, especially education. He synthesized the many suggestions for the schools which came from the experience of the teachers and rectors. Directed by the Third General Congregation, he began the strenuous effort of evaluating the great mass of background material which had accumulated in order to create a comprehensive code on studies. This was later was known as the *Ratio Studiorum.* From the time of Ignatius to the end of Everard's term of office the Society had grown to a little over 5,000 men in 21 provinces, 144 colleges, 10 professed houses, 12 novitiates, and 33 residences. (Ban, Ham, JLx, Som)

S.G. James de Mesquita
(Portuguese: 1553-1614)

Death of James Mesquita

James, a missionary to Japan, brought to Europe four noble envoys chosen by recently converted Japanese princes. Wherever these four noble youths visited they were greeted as royalty. And when they met the king of Portugal it was as if four heads of state had come to Lisbon. Throughout these official visits James served as interpreter for the youths. Rome also celebrated the envoys' entry surrounded by cardinals, bishops, knights and cavalry, as the four young men dressed in their princely ceremonial robes arrived. When James returned to Japan, however, he found that the emperor Hideyoshi had abandoned his sympathy for Christianity and his support of the Jesuits. Instead he banished them from the empire and James died while being sent into exile. (Tan, Tyl)

John   Messari

John - Baptist Messari
(German: 1673-1723)

John was one of four Jesuits martyred during the persecution in Tonkin between 1721 and 1723. It was part of the 100-year effort to suppress Christianity and during that time the native Christians suffered martyrdom by the thousands. (Ham)

Paul and companions

St. Paul Miki
(Japanese: 1564-1597)

Paul was the *first* Japanese member of any Catholic religious order, and had it not been for his martyrdom, he would have been the *first* Japanese priest. After Francis Xavier's death Christianity in Japan developed so rapidly that by 1592 the number of Christians had grown to 200,000. Because several influential political leaders had become converts, and because the rulers had been favorably disposed to Christianity, the Jesuit mission prospered. In 1587, however, this all suddenly changed because the Buddhists feared this increase was a precursor for a Spanish take-over; all missionaries were ordered out of Japan. A few Jesuits obeyed the edict and left the country, but most of them remained and went undercover so as to continue to serve and be with the Catholics as their Jesuit companions had done in England, outwitting - at least for a time - Queen Elizabeth's Inquisition. Paul Miki was the son of a well-to-do Japanese military chief, living near Kyoto, and as such had the right to wear the bright, noble kimono of the Samurai. Even as a Scholastic, before ordination, he proved himself to be an excellent disputant with Buddhist leaders. He was recognized as an eloquent speaker who preached with such fervor and eloquence that he converted many listeners who were not Christians. As an unordained Jesuit scholastic Paul was arrested with two companions. A few weeks later the three Jesuits were crucified along with 23 other Christians. Bystanders described Miki's remarkable composure during this ordeal dressed in his Jesuit cassock (although he had the right to dress as a Samurai) and delivering one last sermon from the cross there in Nagasaki in 1597. Miki was not only the *first* religious but also the *first* martyr of Japan. (Ban, Cor, Ham, JLx, Som, Tyl)

John   Molina
(Chilean: 1740-1829)

John   Molina

John entered the Jesuit o r - der and taught botany at the college in Talca, Chile. There he was able to study Chilean history, culture and geography about which he would later write. In 1768 he had to leave Chile because of the expulsion of the Jesuits from the Spanish territories. After the Suppression he was appointed professor of natural sciences at the Institute of Bologna, where h e wrote most of his works. John described an analogy between living organisms and minerals. He proposed a n idea of the gradual evolution of human beings, thereby anticipating Darwin's theory of evolution. In an 1815 work on nature's three kingdoms (mineral, vegetable and animal) he describes the Creator's plan for a continuous seamless chain of life from mineral life to vegetable life to animal life with no discrete discontinuous steps. Crystalline minerals tend to gather together in preparation for the higher form of vegetable life which then evolve into animal life. John showed unusual insight as well as care to maintain the scientific method, basing his claims on scientific observations. Called a heretic b y some observers, he was ordered by the Archbishop o f Bologna to hand over his findings to a committee of 18 theologians. The latter found no difficulty with John's work and approved publication.

Because of John's work *Compendio della storia geografica naturale e civile del regno del Chile* (Bologna, 1776), John remains the classic author on the natural history of Chile. Two 1967 Chilean stamps honor this Italian Jesuit botanist: one refers to him as the "first scientist of Chile" and the other calls him a "benefactor o f national education". His scientific writings also helped direct Chilean intellectuals away from being overly dependent on Spain. (Ban, Ham, JLx, Som)

Luis de Molina
(Spanish: 1535-1600)

Luis de Molina

Luis was one of the most able of all Jesuit theologians. His book *Concordia liberi arbitrii cum gratiae donis* was attacked by the Dominican theologian, Domingo Baez. Jesuits feared the Dominican teaching would lead to Calvinism while the Dominicans felt the Jesuits leaned toward Pelagianism. Superiors of both sides made heroic efforts to find mutual understanding and charity. Luis attempted to clarify his doctrine and to dispel the misgivings of his adversaries in a work which provoked one of the fiercest and most persistent theological controversies in the post-Reformation Roman Catholic church and gave rise to *Molinism*, a system which attempted to reconcile grace and freewill and which was adopted in its essential points by the Society of Jesus. Luis de Molina's argument can be briefly summarized: "All human beings are endowed with equal and sufficient divine grace without distinction as to their individual merits, and that salvation depends on the sinner's willingness to receive grace". Luis' *Concordia* proved to be the most fateful and provocative work the Society ever published and led to the greatest outpouring of metaphysical and theological energy in the history of modern Catholic thought. The strength of opposition, notably that of the Dominicans, to Molina's doctrine ultimately forced Pope Clement VIII to appoint, in 1598, the "Congregatio de auxiliis" to settle the dispute. Agreement proved impossible; in 1607 Paul V suspended its meetings, and in 1611 forbade all further discussion of the question. (Ban, Ham, JLx, Som)

Henry Morse

(English: 1595-1645)

Henry Morse

Henry was born of Protestant parents, became a Catholic, joined the Jesuits and was sent to the English mission where he worked for four years in a poor district outside London. A plague broke out at the time causing great panic. Henry went around administering the sacraments, finding medicine for the sick and preparing the dead for burial. During this time he himself fell victim to the plague three times. But then he was recognized by priest-hunters, arrested and charged with persuading Protestants to leave their faith. Released because of his work with the plague victims, he returned to his work but in a different area, was arrested several times but escaped. Finally he was caught, brought to Tyburn where he was hanged, drawn and quartered. He spoke to those present at his execution. "I am come hither to die for my religion. I have a secret which highly concerns His Majesty and Parliament to know. The kingdom of England will never be truly blessed until it returns to the Catholic faith and its subjects are all united in one belief under the Bishop of Rome. I pray that my death may be some kind of atonement for the sins of this kingdom." (Ban, Bas, Ham, JLx, Som, Tyl)

Philip Mulcaille

(Irish: 1727-1801)

Philip   Mulcaille

Philip founded schools for poor Irish youngsters and continued to work in them long after the Suppression of the Society. Education was always an integral and prominent element of the Society's mission but the conditions of life in 17th and 18th century Ireland did not allow the Jesuits to run their schools there in the same way as those on the continent. Saint Ignatius had specified in his Constitutions (#451): "Reading and writing should not ordinarily be taught, because the Society was limited in numbers and could not attend to everything." Philip was concerned about basic education, not having the luxury of a ready supply of youngsters who were already able to read and write and take on the challenges of the regular Jesuit curricula. A Protestant Divine, Doctor Blake, described his memories of Philip. "The classic elegance, the attic taste, the chaste refinement, the placid virtue and the Gospel simplicity of . . . the learned and venerable Mulcaille". Philip had continued to work for many years under intense pressure such that, in his own words, "Between a confessional, a pulpit and a school, and the care of a parish and a number of other daily avocations I am day after day at the oar, rowing for life." Among his concerns was the promotion of education for poor girls and he played a large part in encouraging the foundation of the Presentation Convent for this purpose in his parish. (McR)

Jerome   Nadal
(Spanish: 1507-1580)

Jerome Nadal

Jerome was sent by Ignatius
to Italy, Spain, Portugal, Germany and Austria in order to
promulgate the Constitutions
of the Society. He founded
many schools and was an official visitor to a number of
provinces. Jerome undertook
the work of publishing a famous book of pictures to help
in the contemplations of the
Spiritual Exercises. He took
advantage of the newly discovered perspective geometry
which enabled three-dimensional shapes to be displayed in
the two-dimensional pages of books which process helped
bring about the scientific revolution. These pictures
provided photographic accuracy that paved the way for
daVinci's technology and Galileo's science. The early
Jesuits had made the connection between these mechanical
sketches and gospel images. Jerome found highly
motivated artists and printers who knew how to draw
realistic perspective pictures of the gospel stories and
print them in books. Then he found a willing and generous
helper in the Antwerp publisher, Christopher Plantin,
who pledged his effort and his capital. In 1593 appeared
Jerome's book *Evangelicae historiae imagines (Pictures of
the Gospel Stories)* which has been called "One of the most
remarkable Counter-reformation publications of the late
sixteenth century." Charles Sommervogel's Jesuit
Bibliography {Vol. 5 p. 1519} counts 153 engravings in
Jerome's book. Per-spective geometry and art arrived in
China along with Matteo Ricci who carried along Jerome's
Imagines as an aid for teaching the gospel message. Matteo
praised Jerome's work: "This book is of even greater use
than the Bible in the sense that while we are talking to
potential converts, we can also place right in front of their

eyes things that with words alone we would not be able to make clear." With the collaboration of Chinese artists Matteo duplicated Jerome's images, adapting them for a Chinese readership, using oriental facial features. Then he brought these perspective images of science, technology and the gospel stories to the imperial court at Beijing in 1601, hoping to convince the emperor of the truths of Christianity. In doing so, he introduced perspective geometry to the Chinese. (Ban, Ham, JLx, O'M, Som)

Like an engineer's design, the important items in Jerome Nadal's pictures were indentified:

A = Bethlehem

B = Forum

C = Manger

D = Child Jesus

E = Angels

F = Cattle

G = The cave was illuminated by the Light of Christ.

Leonard   Neale
(American: 1747-1817)

Leonard   Neale

Leonard was an educator from a large Maryland family; of seven brothers in the Neale family, six joined the Society. Two died prematurely, but four became priests and Leonard became Baltimore's archbishop succeeding John Carroll. Both were concerned about the restoration of the Jesuits as well as the apostolate of education and took the initiative in starting Georgetown University.

Among the hierarchy there was a serious reevaluation of Clement XIV's decision to suppress the Jesuits. Cardinal Pacca in his Memoirs about his own misinformation and prejudices offers a valuable clue to the Suppression.

> "The Pope (Clement XIV) had had anti-Jesuit masters and teachers who had inculcated maxims and opinions altogether opposed to those of the Society; and everyone knows how deep are the impressions made by early teaching. I, too, had been taught in my youth to nourish against the Order feelings of aversion and hatred which amounted even to fanaticism. Suffice it to say that I was given Pascal's famous Provincial Letters . . . and other books of a similar kind. I was in perfect good faith about these books and had not a shadow of a doubt as to their truth and accuracy."

A great many bishops missed the Society and found, in the aftermath of the French Revolution, how much they needed its special skills and became more impatient than ex-Jesuits for the restoration of the Jesuit Order. In 1788 Leonard drew up a petition for himself and 12 other ex-Jesuits in Maryland to organize a link between themselves and the Jesuits in Russia. After the restoration he considered resigning as bishop to take up again his vocation in the restored Society, but considered more important the needs of the infant American Church. Nevertheless he spent much of his energy trying to accelerate the restoration in spite of his observation about the increasing age of the surviving ex-Jesuits. "All members of the Society here are now grown old, the youngest being past 54. Death, therefore, holds out his threatening rod." (Ban, Ham, JLx, Som)

Francis Neumayr
(German: 1697-1765)

Francis Neumayr

Francis was an indefatigable rhetoric and drama teacher, preacher, and moderator of sodalities in Munich. He kept up the dramatic tradition by staging annually productions of the Munich Sodality which he produced in two large volumes, under the title *The Drama of Asceticism*. He also published more than 100 other works on spiritual subjects, some with engaging titles as *Melancholy's Remedy* and The *Uprooting of Sloth*. (Ban, Ham, JLx, Som)

John   Nidhard
(Austrian: 1607-1681)

John Nidhard

John was confessor to Mariana of Austria, the queen mother to the four-year-old Charles II of Spain. Foolishly, she made John a member of the Council of State, the inquisitor general, and in effect, the prime minister. It was a position that was embarrassing to John who felt at home only with philosophy and canon law. It was a bigger problem for the Society. John did not have the qualities needed to be head of state, and being an Austrian was suspect in the eyes of the Spanish people. Don John of Austria came to the rescue by causing such an uproar against this foreigner John Nidhard, that he left Spain, moved to Rome where he made a cardinal by Pope Clement X. (Ban, Ham, JLx, Som)

Eusebio Nieremberg
(Spanish: 1595-1658)

Eusebio

Eusebio taught philosophy and theology in Madrid. He was an author of very influential spiritual tracts and books and perhaps the best known of his 56 works was his 1640 book Time *and Eternity* which has been compared to John Gerson's *The Imitation of Christ*. Eusebio's classic is known popularly by the author's first name: "The Eusebio". (Ban, Ham, JLx, Som)

St. Robert de Nobili

(Italian: 1577-1656)

Robert de Nobili

Robert was a brilliant member of the Roman nobility who was sent to work in Madurai in India. He quickly learned Tamil and adapted himself to the Indian culture. As a nobleman he was judged the equivalent of an Indian rajah, which enabled him to move about with much more freedom than other missionaries. He convinced the Roman authorities that his many converts should not be forced to abandon the signs of their caste. In 1613 a Portuguese provincial superior, unsympathetic to his methods ordered him to cease baptizing, but this edict was later countermanded by Superior General Aquaviva. The storm did not end there, however, and in 1618 a bishops' conference in Goa again condemned Robert. This decision was overturned by Pope Gregory XV who approved Robert's methods. After 39 years of work among the people of Madurai he witnessed the number of Christians grow from zero to more than 4,000. (Ban, Ham, JLx, Som, Tyl)

Robert and a Brahmin friend

Emmanuel   Nobrega
(Portuguese: 1517-1570)

Emmanuel was a remarkable missionary who first encountered the
natives of Bahia and São Paulo
with four Jesuit companions. He is
called Brazil's greatest early political figure. Upon his arrival in
the New World, he told his companions: "This land is our enterprise".   The daring and optimism

Emmanuel   Nobrega

of the Brazilian Mission were read in the sails of his ship:
Unus non sufficit orbis (One world is not big enough). He
also founded Salvador in Bahia in 1549 and with Bl. Joseph
Anchieta, S.J. co-founded São Paulo in 1554 and Rio de
Janeiro in 1565. He also established colleges that were
giving Master's degrees by 1578. (Ban, DSB, JLx, O'M, Som)

Com. stamp honoring Emmanuel

Charles de Noyelle
(French: 1615-1686)

Charles de Noyelle

Charles was the 12th Superior General of the Society and the only one of the 29 generals between the term of Ignatius Loyola and the present Superior General, Kolvenbach, who was chosen unanimously. He held the office for only four years, but these were terribly agonizing years. He had to endure continual and merciless pressure from the Spanish Hapsburgs and the French Bourbons, the latter pressure was intensified by the Jesuit confessor of Louis XIV, François de la Chaize. When Louis XIV ordered that the Gallican Articles be taught in all Jesuit colleges attached to universities Charles wrote emphatically to François de la Chaize: "Never shall I permit a Jesuit to teach anything disapproved by the supreme pontiff." (Ban, Ham, JLx, Som)

St. John Ogilvie
(Scottish: 1579-1615)

John Ogilvie

John is the Church's only officially recorded Scottish martyr. Since his father had conformed to the state-established religion, young John was brought up a Calvinist. Upon reaching his 17th year, he determined to become a Catholic and went to Louvain, Belgium, where he was reconciled with the Catholic Church. He later joined the Jesuits and was ordained in Paris in 1610. Sent to work in Rouen, he kept importuning the Superior General to send him back to Scotland in response to the entreaty for Jesuits from the Earl of Angus to the Jesuit General: "Send only those who wish for this mission and are strong enough to bear the heat of the day for they will be in exceeding danger." In earlier times wholesale massacres of Catholics had taken place in Scotland but at this time the hunt concentrated on priests and on those who attended their Masses. The Jesuits were determined not to abandon the Catholic laity, but to be with them and provide the consolation of the sacraments. When captured they were tortured for information, then hanged, and, while still alive, taken down and their limbs pulled out and finally cut up into quarters and each part placed on one of the four city gates.

At last Ogilvie's request was granted and he returned to his native Scotland in 1613 to begin a brief missionary career that lasted only 11 months and ended in martyrdom. In Edinburgh and Glasgow he worked underground avoiding the Queen's priest-hunters, disguised as a soldier by the name of Watson. Ogilvie was captured and put in prison where he showed his interrogators that he was not to be bullied into acknowledging the King's supremacy in religious matters. He refused to divulge the names of the Catholics who had attended his Masses, so they applied an extreme measure of torture. He annoyed his tormentors by not crying out in pain and in fact meeting their cruelty with humor. "I make no account of you and can willingly suffer more for this cause than you are able to inflict. Your threats cheer me; I mind them no more than the cackling of geese." Asked if he feared to die he said: "No more than you do to dine." No relic of his body remains. (Ban, Bas, Cor, Ham, JLx, Som, Tyl)

Death of Edward Oldcorne

Bl. Edward Oldcorne
(English: 1561-1606)

Edward labored in the English mission in Worcestershire for 16 years where many came to him for encourage-ment. He developed can-cer of the throat, but he kept preaching even though it was quite pain-ful. Edward made a pil-grimage to St. Winifred's shrine in Flintshire to seek a cure which was granted and his cancer was healed. He returned stronger and healthier than before. Then he fell victim to the "Gunpowder Plot" which was a foolish conspiracy to blow up the king and parliament. It was hatched by a small group of Catholic Englishmen who were frustrated by their Protestant rulers; all it did was provide an opportunity to renew persecution of Catholics and thereby to involve Jesuits. Edward was arrested, falsely accused and placed on the rack for five days to find names of the perpetrators and sympathizers in the plot. The rack master got no information. Edward was hanged and quartered along with another Jesuit, Brother Ralph Ashley. (Ban, Bas, Tan, Tyl)

John Paul Oliva
(Italian: 1600-1681)

John Paul Oliva

John was the 11th Superior General of the Society. John Paul loved the fine arts; he identified the Jesuits of Rome with the fullness of the baroque style. He sponsored three great artistic achievements: the completion of the church of Sant' Andrea al Quirinale; the adornment of the interior of the Gesù Church and in the decoration of Saint Ignatius Church. The great artist, Giovanni Lorenzo Bernini, and John Paul Oliva were close personal friends and Bernini provided a number of illustrations for an edition of John Paul's sermons. Given a free hand at Sant' Andrea, Bernini created one of the most beautiful baroque churches in Rome. John Paul then commissioned Giovanni Battista Gaulli to decorate the austere Gesù where Gaulli produced a magnificent fresco on the ceiling *The Triumph of the Holy Name of Jesus*. Brother Andrea Pozzo painted the spectacular perspective painting of the worldwide Jesuit apostolate on the ceiling of Saint Ignatius Church. (Ban, Ham, JLx, Som)

St. Nicholas Owen

(English: ?-1606)

Death of Nicholas Owen

Nicholas was a Coadjutor Brother who was a mason and carpenter by trade, and who used these talents creatively in the service of the persecuted Church in England. His ingenuity saved hundreds of priests from capture by the persistent bounty hunters operating during the Elizabethan inquisition. Nicholas' cleverness provided priests with safe refuge from these priest-hunters. Of his three brothers, two became priests and one became a printer of underground Catholic books who provided material for the Jesuits. Nicholas' early Jesuit companion was Edmund Campion and Nicholas was arrested when he spoke openly of Campion's innocence. Nicholas later was released; he then contacted Henry Garnet and became his associate. In time the priest hunters got to know Nicholas as "Garnet's man", while the priests knew him as "Little John". Nicholas constructed hiding places in the various mansions used as priest-centers throughout England. During the day he worked on either the interior or the exterior of the building, but always in public view so that the servants would think that he was a hired carpenter. During the evening and night, however, he worked on his concealed rooms, digging deep into the earth or chipping through thick stone walls. He always worked alone to insure secrecy. Only he and the owner of the house knew where the secret rooms were located. Nicholas had no formal novitiate, but he received his religious training in his close collaboration with his superior. In 1594, he was helping John Gerard in a London residence when both were arrested and taken to the Counter prison. Nicholas was still unknown as the mastermind behind the hiding places and was considered but a small fish in the vast ocean of Catholic disobedience. He was released and immediately returned to his inventive labors. Eventually Nicholas was again captured and brought to the Tower for intense torture so that the priest hunters could learn the location of his many hiding places. His silence infuriated his tormentors who increased his unspeakable suffering until it caused his death. The Elizabethan inquisitors learned nothing from him. John Gerard said of Nicholas that no other Jesuit had rendered such valuable service to the Catholic cause in England, "since, through his skill and ingenuity in devising places of concealment, he had saved the lives of hundreds of people." (Ban, Bas, Cor, JLx, Tyl)

One of Nicholas' "priest holes"

Bl. Francis Pacheco
(Portugal: 1565-1626)

Francis & companions

Francis was a missionary to China and Japan. On his third entrance into Japan in disguise, Francis was captured by the Shogun's many spies and put in a prison with other Jesuits, catechists, and lay people. Among them were some young men preparing to enter the Society, and, with martyrdom imminent, Pacheco permitted them to make their vows. In 1626 they all suffered martyrdom at Nagasaki. Francis was the most experienced of all the 33 Jesuits who were martyred in Japan during the great persecution between 1617 and 1626. During these terrible years he saw thousands of Christians deny their Faith for fear of torture but he also saw thousands endure the death by slow fire. There during the next six months he formed a quasi-religious community of the fellow prisoners with regular periods of fast and prayers to strengthen themselves against the inevitable ordeal ahead. The laymen were taken last in the hopes that they would change their minds, but they were only strengthened in their resolve. (Cor, Ham, JLx, Som, Tyl)

Peter Páez

(Spanish: 1564-1622)

Peter Páez

Peter was a missionary to Ethiopia. This favorite mission of Ignatius took a heavy toll of Jesuit lives and had a tragic ending. During its 85-year history, 1554-1639, 20 of the 56 Jesuits who tried to enter the country perished. Upon his arrival, Peter was captured by Muslims and condemned to six years in galleys. During this time he learned several languages. Peter entered Ethiopia a second time disguised as an Armenian merchant and then worked as a stone-mason. He composed a two-volume history of Ethiopia, and is said to have been the first European to reach the sources of the Nile. Eventually he was received into the court of the Negus, Za-Denghal, whom he converted. This ruler, however, was assassinated shortly after his conversion. Then Paez convinced the next Negus, Socinios, that Monophysitism (only one nature in Christ) was inconsistent with Christianity. When Socinios announced his conviction of the two natures in Christ, a revolt spread throughout the country thus endangering the promulgation of Catholic doctrine in Ethiopia and the reunion of the Abyssinian church with Rome. A Catholic Patriarch was sent from Rome to work with the now-Catholic Socinios to make the union with Rome succeed, but after the deaths of Paez and Socinios the succeeding negus forbade any more contact with Rome. This had less to do with adhesion to any theological convictions than to the very pragmatic fact that independence from Rome meant that this new negus was free to keep his harem and also that the leading merchants and politicians of Ethiopia would experience no restraint upon their tradition of polygamy. Up to this time resentments had been smoldering, but the new negus openly unleashed the fierce opposition to the prospect of the country's leaders being forced to adhere to the strict Catholic moral code. During the transition two Jesuits were stabbed to death, five hanged and the Patriarch fled the country. (Ban, JLx, Som)

Bl. Francis Page
(Belgian: ?-1602)

Francis was born into a wealthy Protestant family, studied law and became a clerk for a Catholic lawyer. Francis fell in love with his employer's daughter, but she would not hear of marriage until Francis became a Catholic. He knew John Gerard, S.J. who was in London's Clink Prison at the time. He went to John for in-struction, called off the marriage

Death of Francis Page

and decided to become a Jesuit. After ordination he returned to England, managed to elude the priest-hunters for a few years but was captured and brought to Newgate prison. Philip pointed out that he did not come under England's law since he was born in Antwerp not in England. Nevertheless he was found guilty of high treason and condemned to be hanged, drawn and quartered. (Bas, Tan, Tyl)

Peter Sforza Pallavicino
(Italian: 1607-1667)

Peter Sforza Pallavicino

Peter brought distinction to the staff of the Roman College as an eminent historian and theologian. He held the chair of theology at the Roman College but is remembered more for his *History of the Council of Trent* (1653) than for his theological works. Pope Innocent X had requested Peter to write the Council's history in order to correct previous hostile versions. It took him five years of research in the Vatican archives to write his two volume work, after which he was made a cardinal. (Ban, Ham, JLx, Som)

Dominic Parrenin

(French: 1618-1679)

Dominic   Parrenin

Dominic in collaboration with five other Jesuit cartographers constructed the famous 1735 "Jesuit Map" of China, Manchuria, and Mongolia. Some emperors, because of their respect for the learned Jesuits, allowed Jesuits to live in China and maintain a church. Even during the persecution of the Church Jesuits such as Dominic were allowed to continue their work. Possessing a robust constitution, a dignified and majestic appearance, a facility with the different Chinese dialects, a vigorous spirit, an amazing memory and prodigious amount of learning Dominic labored in China for 43 years. (Ban, Ham, JLx, Som)

Peter   Pázmany
(Hungarian: 1570-1637)

Peter   Pázmany

Peter   was   known   as   *the creator   of   the   philosophical and   theological   language   of Hungary.*   His   sermons   were said   to   have   been   very moving   and   his   writings have   become   a   landmark   in the   history   of   Hungarian literature.   Both   Hungary   and Czechoslovakia   claim   him, and   often   compete   with   each other   in   honoring   him   with commemorative   stamps.   He was   the   founder   of   the   *Jesuit University   of   Trnava,*   which was   the   first   Hungarian university.   It   is   claimed   as an   original   foundation   both by   Trnava   University   located in   Czechoslovakia   and   the   University   of   Budapest   located   in Hungary.

The   Jesuits   worked   in   Hungary   from   the   earliest   years of   the   Society,   from   1561.   There   were   three   early   Jesuit versions   of   *Peter   the   Great*:   Peter   Canisius   in   Germany, Peter   Skarga   in   Poland   and   Peter   Pázmány   in   Hungary. The   latter,   preserved   the   Faith   in   his   country   according   to the   Catholic   Encyclopedia.   "By   far   the   greatest   figure   of the   age   was   Peter   Cardinal   Pázmany,   S.J.,   a   former Protestant   who   became   Catholicism's   most   zealous   and   most brilliant   leader.   Almost   single-handedly   he   reconverted the   greater   part   of   Hungary   to   Catholicism."   Just   when whole   families   were   leaving   the   Church   he   came   to   the rescue.   He   created   a   philosophical   and   theological language   for   Hungary.   In   1616   Pope   Paul   V   circumvented the   Jesuit   prohibition   against   ecclesiastical   honors   and made   Peter   Pázmány   Cardinal   and   the   primate   of   Hungary. Peter   entrusted   to   his   fellow   Jesuits   two   colleges,   a university   and   a   seminary.

By the time the Society was suppressed in 1773 the Hungarian province numbered 1,000 men in 52 houses, directing 32 colleges and 7 Centers of Higher Education. After the Suppression most of these schools continued to operate some were taken over by the government and some by other Religious Orders. Jesuits had labored for a long time in an area devastated and sacked for 150 years by the Turks and divided by religious wars. Still carrying on Peter's legacy, in this century the Hungarian Jesuits labored to prepare an elite core of Catholic intellectuals as part of a wider campaign to check the spread of totalitarianism and anti-religious teaching. (Ban, Ham, JLx, Som)

Com. stamp of Peter Pázmany

Robert   Persons
(English: 1546-1610)

Robert   Persons

Robert had to give up his teaching position at Oxford University, because he was a Catholic. He left England, entered the Society of Jesus and returned to England in disguise to assist the persecuted Catholics. He was especially irritated at the humiliating policy that the Catholics had to send their children to Protestant schools at their own expense. Robert became one of the foremost English Jesuits in the late 16th century. He had managed to escape back to the continent after the arrest of Edmund Campion; then he went to Spain in 1588, where he founded several seminaries for the training of English priests and was active at the court of Philip II. Written under the pseudonym 'Philopater', his *responsio* (response) attacked the proclamation of Queen Elizabeth condemning Jesuits for trying to reinstate the Catholic Faith in England. Robert directed his invective against the Queen herself and elaborated on the pope's power to depose heretical sovereigns. It was because of this that his *responsio* is usually regarded as the most extreme evidence of exile opposition to Elizabeth and of the policies of those who believed that the hope of Catholicism in England depended on foreign intervention. When he returned to England he experienced the efficiency of the English government spy system, was captured and executed. (Ban, Bas, Cor, Ham, JLx, Som)

Dennis   Petau
(French: 1583-1652)

Dennis   Petau

Dennis was a prince among scholars: he had mastered   Latin   and Greek at the age of 15 and defended in Greek his thesis for the Paris master's degree at 17. After entering the Society he taught rhetoric at Reims, La Flèche, and Paris. When he approached his main task, teaching   theology,   he brought together all his skills along with a profound knowledge of Sacred Scripture. He had so a wide a familiarity with the Fathers of the Church and councils that he has been called the *Father of Positive Theology*. His five volume work *Theological Doctrines* is considered a masterpiece, as he was willing to modestly admit in a letter to Superior General Vitelleschi. "In this treatise on things divine I have not followed the road trod by the old school. I have taken a new road, and I can say without pride, a road as yet untouched by any other. Putting aside that subtle kind of theology which meanders, like philosophy, through I do not know what labyrinths, I have created a simple, graceful venture, like a rapid stream, from the pure and original sources of Scripture, the councils and the Fathers." (Ban, Ham, JLx, Som)

Ignatius   Pickel
(German: 1736-1818)

Ignatius   Pickel

Ignatius   was   a   scientist   who taught   at   the   university   in Dillingen.   After   the   Suppres-sion   the   University   of   Mann-heim   offered   him   the   chair   of astronomy.   The   archbishop   of Eystadt   wanted   him   to   work   in his   diocese   and   gave   him   a professorship   in   mathematics. In   this   position   he   was   in charge   of   the   department   of physics   and   the   museum   of natural   history. (DSB, Ham, JLx, Som)

St.   Joseph Pignatelli
(Italian: 1737-1811)

Joseph   Pignatelli

Joseph   led   and   inspired   the Jesuits   in   exile   during   their   41 years   of   the   Suppression   and   is considered   the   link   between   the old   Society,   suppressed   in   1773, and   the   new   Society,   restored   in 1814. He had   entered   the   Society in   Spain   in   1753   and   experienced the   terrible   blow   of   the   edict expelling   the   Jesuits   from   Spain in 1767. No explanation   for   the   outrage   was   offered;   the reason   for   their   banishment   given   by   King   Charles   III   was "kept   locked   in   our   royal   bosom."   Although   he   was   offered the opportunity to remain in Spain because of his noble birth, Joseph stayed with his exiled Jesuits on their torturous journeys through Europe. As they moved, they found that the Jesuits were being expelled gradually from all countries except Prussia and Russia. Joseph was persistent in keeping together a remnant who would eventually witness the restoration of the Society in 1814, three years after Joseph's death.

The Society was never really completely suppressed and continued to thrive in Russia. Joseph associated himself with the Jesuits in Russia, but remained living in Italy. In 1775 Pius VI gave permission for Jesuits from other countries to rejoin the order in Russia and in 1799 approved the opening of a novitiate in Colorno (Italy), making Joseph Pignatelli the Master of Novices. In 1801 Charles Emmanuel IV of Sardinia reinstated the Jesuits in his kingdom and he himself joined the Jesuits 14 years later. Also groups of Jesuits had reformed into societies such as *The Society of the Sacred Heart of Jesus* in France and *The Society of the Faith of Jesus* in Italy. From 1800 the new Pope Pius VII was determined to complete the restoration of the Society but was not able until the fall of Napoleon. On the octave day of the feast of St. Ignatius (the Papal Bull could not prepared in time for the feast itself) the Pope came to celebrate Mass at the church of the Jesu and, in the presence of many cardinals and about 100 Jesuits (very old men from the old Society and very young men who had just entered), promulgated the Bull restoring the Society. In spite of the fact that virtually nothing was left of the Society's resources, requests for the restored Jesuits to start schools poured in from every direction. Within a year the Society had as many members and as many foundations as the old Society had had in 1555. (Ban, Cor, Ham, JLx, Som, Tyl)

Suppression in Spain

St. Stephen Pongrácz

(Transylvanian: 1583-1619)

Stephen Pongrácz 1

Stephen was one of the three *Martyrs of Kosice* put to death at the hands of fanatical Calvinists along with Melchior Grodecz and Mark Crisinus, who was the Cathedral Canon in Kosice. Stephen could have lived an honorable pleasant life in his native Transylvania, but chose to preach the Gospel in eastern Slovakia. When he preached in Kosice, Hungary, he was granted the palm of martyrdom, which he had always considered a most enviable reward. A Calvinist prince in Transylvania was taking advantage of Hungary's involvement in the 30-year war and tried to expand his own territory. At that time Kosice was a stronghold of Hungarian Calvinists, and the few Catholics who lived in the city and its outlying districts had been without a priest for some time. Melchior Grodecz came to help the Polish speaking Catholics and Stephen Pongrácz came for those who spoke a Slavic language or German. When the Calvinist Minister heard the Jesuits had arrived he sent his soldiers to arrest them. Stephen, Melchior and Mark were then brutally tortured and killed. The Calvinists refused to allow the remaining Catholic citizens to bury them until three months had passed. Tenacious as were the Calvinists in their hold on much of this unhappy country they could not halt the creation of a powerful Catholic bastion there. (Ban, Cor, Ham, JLx, Som, Tyl)

Charles Porée

(French: 1675-1741)

Charles   Porée

Charles   taught   literature at the   college   of   Louis-le-Grand   and   inspired   his students   to   brilliant   use   of their   own   language   with-out minimizing   the   classi-cal authors.   He was   a bril-liant   dramatist   continuing the   Jesuit   tradition   of drama.   Goethe   wrote   re-garding   Jesuit   drama: "This   public   performance has   again   convinced   me   of the   cleverness   of   the Jesuits.   They   despised nothing   which   could in   any   way   be   effective,   and   treated the   matter   with   love   and   attention.   Just   as   this   great religious   society   counts   among   its   numbers   organ-builders,   sculptors   and   painters,   so   are   there   some   also   who devote   themselves   with   knowledge   and   inclination   to the theater,   and   in   the   same   manner   in   which   they distinguish   their   churches   by   a pleasing   magnificence, these   intelligent   men   here   have   made   themselves   masters of   the   worldly   senses   by   means   of   a theater   worthy   of respect."   Charles   was   one   of   the   most   important   Jesuit dramatist   of that   period   and his   dramas   were   compared   to those   of   Moliere.   Jesuit   theater   was   quite   influential   in the development   of   drama,   educating   Diderot,   Moliere   and Corneille.   Charles   Porée   taught   Voltaire   who   spent   seven years   with   the   Jesuits.   In   later   years   Charles   was   a good friend   of   Voltaire   who   found   in   the   Jesuits   a sympathetic spirit   in   contrast   to   the   dismal   fanaticism   of   the   Jansenists. For   his   whole   life   Voltaire   maintained   friendly   relations with   his   former   teachers,   especially   with   Charles   Porée. (Ban, Ham, JLx, Som)

Antonio
Possevino
(Italian: 1533-1611)

Antonio   Possevino

Antonio was charged b y
the   popes   with   v e r y
sensitive   diplomatic
missions,   not   all   o f
which   were   successful.
In   1577,   following
Stanislaus   Warszewicki,
S.J. whose   story   is   told
elsewhere, Antonio w a s
sent   to   Sweden   in   t h e
time   of   the   L u t h e r a n
King   III,   who   w a s
married   to   the   Catholic
Princess Catherine of Poland, in the hope of winning t h e
country   to   the   Catholic   Faith.   King   John   was   quite
interested but had four conditions: a married clergy, Holy
Communion   under   both   species   and   Mass   in   t h e
vernacular. Most importantly, he wanted the conversion of
his people to be a gradual process. Antonio presented t h e
king's plan to the Roman Curia who refused to grant t h e s e
requested dispensations. It seemed that at the time J o h n ' s
gradualism   would   have   worked   in   Sweden   where   t h e
Catholic faith was still very much alive if only Rome h a d
granted   the   dispensations   he   requested.   If   Antonio   h a d
been heeded Sweden might have become a great Catholic
outpost of the North. Instead the opportunity was lost.

   After his discouraging   experience in Sweden, he w a s
sent by Pope Gregory XIII to the court of Ivan the T e r r i b l e
who claimed to be interested   in discussing what s e v e r a l
previous   popes   had   tried   to   establish   - relations   w i t h
Russia. Actually Ivan, doing poorly in his war with Poland,
sought   papal   intervention   to   mediate   the   dispute   a n d
offered the attractive assurance that he would open h i s
country   to   the   West.   Pope   Gregory   XIII   grasped   t h i s
opportunity   and   assigned   Antonio   to   begin   a n o t h e r
exercise in diplomacy which was bound to fail. Behind h i s

facade of good will Ivan hid his real objective of merely halting Poland's military success. Nothing more interested him. When Antonio and Ivan came to the crux of the papal mission, the question of church unity, Ivan erupted into a fearful outburst of rage. Over Antonio he waved his scepter with which he had killed his son not long before. Through it all Antonio stood up to this terrible man quietly and calmly. The goal of religious accord between Rome and Moscow remained elusive, but when the war between Russia and Poland came to a stalemate and a negotiated peace was at hand, both parties immediately agreed that Antonio Possevino should take part in the peace conference as president and neutral arbitrator. Thus was achieved one of the greatest triumphs of Jesuit diplomacy. Two powerful monarchs had placed their fates confidently in the hands of a Jesuit priest, and looked to him, as the authorized agent of the pope, for a just decision.

Often Antonio had occasion to carry out a variety of diplomatic missions in other parts of the world on behalf of Rome. He enjoyed the confidence of the pope as well as of the Hapsburg monarch, of the Archdukes of Graz and Vienna as well as of the Great Council of Venice. He was acquainted with the innermost aspirations of all the leaders of Europe; he was fully informed of the financial situation of every government; he knew the military strength of every country, and, accordingly, was able to pursue diplomacy in the grand style.

Even in Poland too, Antonio, in company with his fellow-Jesuit, Peter Skarga, worked energetically towards the strengthening of the Catholic faith, and not only concerned himself with the establishment of further Jesuit colleges, with the appointment of bishops and the training of the future priests, but also with the setting up of printing-presses and the publication of the Catholic catechism in both Polish and Lithuanian. He attached particular importance to the winning over to Rome of the Ruthenians. Since they were under Polish domination, the Catholic Church was free to develop among them without hindrance under the protection of King Stephen; after the Ruthenians had been converted, Antonio's object was to take advantage of their national kinship with the Russians by using them as Catholic animators in Russia. Similarly, Antonio saw in the Baltic provinces, which were again under the dominion of Poland, a further bridge across which Catholicism might penetrate into Russia, and accordingly he vigorously promoted the Catholic cause i n those lands. The value of Antonio's personality and of his work for Catholicism cannot therefore, in any sense, be gauged merely by those of his great achievements which are immediately apparent; it reveals itself rather, on more than one occasion, in the developments of much later times.   (Ban,   Ham, JLx, O'M, Som)

**Anthony at the side of
King Stephen Batory
of Poland in 1576**

An extra glimpse of the early Society

Jan Kasimierz, brother of King Ladislaus IV of Poland, entered a Jesuit novitiate in 1643. He left the Jesuit order two years later and then was made a cardinal in 1647. In 1648 became King of Poland. He began an agonizing and tragic reign lasting 20 turbulent years, marked by civil and military reversals. In 1668 he abdicated and spent the rest of his life in a monastery.

Andrea   Pozzo
(Italian: 1640-1709)

Andrea Pozzo

Andrea was a Jesuit Co-adjutor Brother who made remarkable contributions to perspective geometry. Andrea wrote one of the earliest books on perspectivities "meant to aid artists and architects". Some of his principles of perspectivity have found their way into modern movies. His book has gone into many editions, even into this century, and has been translated from· the original Latin and Italian into numerous languages such as French, German, English and Chinese. Andrea is famous for his perspective decorative work in Genoa, Turin and Milan, but is best known for his perspective paintings on the ceiling of St. Ignatius Church in Rome. Here there are three masterful applications of his perspective art. A cupola was in the original plans for this church, but without the funds it had to be omitted leaving only a yawning gap in a flat ceiling. On this gap Pozzo was asked to apply his perspective art and construct a virtual dome on a flat piece of canvas. He finished this project in nine months. Large crowds who came for the feast of St. Ignatius in 1685, were astonished to see a vaulted cupola with several tiers of columns. They could not believe that the ceiling was flat. When asked if he had too many tiers of columns, he replied: "When my brackets give way and my columns start to fall, you will find painters among my friends who will remake them better." Next came the apse, where he depicted scenes from the life of Ignatius. His rendering of Ignatius' vision at La Storta is referred to as: "one of the dominant notes of the art of Catholic reform."

Andrea presented astonishing perspective ceiling paintings along the massive vault of the church. His theme is the missionary spirit of the Society. Light comes from God the Father to the Son who transmits it to St. Ignatius as it breaks into four rays leading to the four continents. The beautiful ceiling celebrates two centuries of adventuresome Jesuit explorers and missionaries. (Ban, DSB, Ham, JLx, Som)

Andrea's altar of Ignatius at the JESU church in Rome

René Rapin
(French: 1621-1687)

René Rapin

René was a Latin poet who was known as the second Theocritus because his works were comparable to masters of the Augustan age. He was even more prolific as an essayist in the French language. One major division of his work was literary criticism. His most noteworthy efforts here are *Observations on the Poems of Horace and Virgil* and *Reflections on the Poetics of Aristotle and on the Works of the Poets, Ancient and Modern* (1676). As especially the first title indicates, René favored comparisons of the classical Greek and Roman authors; between Demosthenes and Cicero, Plato and Aristotle, and Thucydides and Livy. These comparisons were also translated into English as early as the 17th century. In the fields of ascetical theology and controversial literature, René's chief works were *The Spirit of Christianity* (1672) and *The Perfection of Christianity* (1673). Although a lifelong foe of the Jansenists, René's chief controversial works were not published until the 19th century. One of his editors ascribes the reason for René's reluctance to publishing these works during his lifetime to René's desire to spare the families of those attacked in the works. His two posthumous works are *History of Jansenism*, and *Memoirs on the Church, Society, the Court, the City, and Jansenism*. Despite the late appearance in print of these works, René's chief place in theology was his role as antagonist to the Jansenists. René had a long and fruitful career as poet, literary critic, and controversial theologian. (Ban, Ham, JLx, JLP, Som)

St. Bernadine Realino

(Italian: 1530-1616)

Bernadine was known as the patron and apostle of the Town of Lecci. He had studied law and medicine at Bologna and had a successful government career. Then he entered the Society, worked in Naples and later was sent to Lecci to found a college. There he quickly became the most loved man in Lecci because of his concern and charity. He made himself appear the receiver rather than the giver, and the poor

Bernadine   Realino

had a special claim on his services. One of the more interesting miracles attributed to him concerned his small pitcher of wine which did not give out until everyone present had had enough. (Ban, Cor, Ham, JLx, Som, Tyl)

Postmark of Francis Regis used in Le Puy

St. John Francis Regis

(French: 1597-1640)

John Francis Regis

John was a home missionary to southern France, visiting hospitals and prisons, reviving the faith of lax Catholics, assisting the needy, and bringing the hope of Christ to the poor. His influence reached all classes and brought about a lasting and profound spiritual revival throughout France.

When he became a Jesuit, he requested the mission of evangelizing the fallen-away Cath-olics of the interior of France which still suffered from the sad effects of the Wars of Religion - that civil strife between French Calvinists and Catholics. Since a good portion of southern France had been under the control of the Huguenots, the Catholics in those areas had been forced to abandon the practice of their faith. Their churches had been destroyed and their priests slain. Now that peace returned to the country, it was the task of the home missionary to rekindle the faith that had once been there. John traveled through many towns, even climbing difficult mountains, to carry God's message. He consoled the disturbed of heart, visited prisons, collected clothing and food for the poor, and established homes for prostitutes so that they might be rehabilitated. His influence reached all classes and brought about a lasting spiritual revival throughout France. Numerous miraculous cures of the sick effected during his lifetime continued to occur after John's death. Many institutions are named after John Francis Regis. (Ban, Cor, Ham, JLx, Som, Tyl)

Francis   Retz

(Yugoslav: 1673-1750)

Francis   Retz

Francis became the 15th Superior General of the Society at the age of 57 with all but two out of 78 votes cast in the Sixteenth General Congregation. During Francis' term of office Benedict XIV was known for the breadth of his learning. It was he who reluctantly brought to an end the controversies about the Chinese and Malabar rites. Because of the decision made by the Congregation for the Propagation of the Faith, the Jesuits in China were forced to abandon their practice of adapting the Gospel message to the culture of the Chinese; the decision squandering a courageous and successful mode of evangelization and missing a rare opportunity for the spread of the Church. (Ban, Ham, JLx, Som)

Alexander Rhodes
(French: 1591-1660)

Alexander   Rhodes

Alexander worked in Indo-china, an area very respon-sive to the faith. His contin-ual preaching illustrated how well he had mastered the language and the cus-toms of the people. He also left behind accounts of his travels which are precious historical documents for Vietnam. Alexander was a linguist who transcribed the Vietnamese (Indochinese) language into Latin, wrote a Latin-Vietnamese catechism, a Vietnamese-Latin-Portuguese lexicon and a grammar of the native language. He was carrying on an invaluable Jesuit tradition, there being about 40 languages in the world that were first transcribed by Jesuits missionaries.

Alexander insisted on the development of a native clergy and soon afterwards 300,000 natives received baptism in spite of the fact that the governors were hostile toward Christianity. He labored in the area of Hue and Danang from 1640 until 1645. It was Alexander's broad vision which inspired a new missionary orientation: the creation of vicars apostolic, aided by diocesan priests, directly under the Holy See and independent of the Portuguese colonial system. The Congregation of Propaganda instructed the new vicars apostolic to respect the customs of the natives. De Rhodes gave tremendous impetus to the onward sweep of the Church in Indo-China in spite of the fact that the civil authorities had taken a hostile attitude toward Christianity. He formed catechists who gave remarkable support to the Christians, especially in times of persecutions. In 1660 Alexander died in Ispahan, the capital of Persia, deeply respected and mourned by the Shah. His tomb, however, is in Vietnam where he is known as "The First Father". This title is commemorated in a 1960 Vietnam stamp because of his innovations concerning the Vietnamese language. (Ban, DSB, Ham, JLx, Som)

Com. stamp honors Alexander's contributions to the language

Peter Ribadeneyra
(Spanish: 1527-1611)

Peter was one of the early companions, renowned for his writings which included the Life of St. Ignatius and a bibliography of Jesuit writings. It was he who, with patient diplomacy at the Court of Philip II, received the reluctant approval for Jesuit activities from the government of the Netherlands. (Ban, Ham, JLx, O'M, Som)

Peter Ribadeneyra

Laurence Ricci

(Italian: 1703-1775)

Laurence Ricci

Laurence was the 18th Superior General and had to endure the ordeal of the Suppression of the Society. For 15 years he had to cope with the terrible opposition to the Society and saw the Society gradually being dismembered and eventually crushed. After the edict was carried out he was imprisoned. Even though he was over 70, he was kept in the prison of Castel Sant' Angelo, deprived of reading and writing materials as well as ordinary amenities such as heat (even in the dead of winter) and was allowed to talk to no one, not even to his cell guards. He lasted only a few years under these dreadful conditions: conditions imposed by Pope Clement XIV; conditions which illustrated how deep-seated was the hatred of those who conspired in the Suppression of the Society. (Ban, Ham, JLx, Som)

Castel Sant'Angelo where Laurence was imprisoned by Clement XIV and where Laurence died.

Matteo   Ricci
(Italian: 1552-1610)

Matteo   Ricci

Matteo entered the Jesuits against the wishes of his father who forbade any talk of religious topics around the home. When his father came to take Matteo out of the Jesuit novitiate, the father was stricken ill. He took this as a sign that his son Matteo truly had a vocation, and that it would be better for both Matteo and himself for Matteo to remain a Jesuit. Matteo was sent to China in 1583 and worked there for 27 years. He was welcomed to the academies and gained many influential friendships. When the time was ripe, he opened a residence in Nanking for himself, his fellow Jesuits and his scientific instruments. Eventually he became the court mathematician in Peking. His books *Geometrica Practica* and *Trigonometrica* were translations of Clavius' works into Chinese. He made Western developments in mathematics available to the Chinese and published in 1584 and 1600 the first two maps of China ever available to the West. For the first time the Chinese had an idea of the distribution of oceans and land masses. He introduced trigonometric and astronomical instruments, and translated the first six books of Euclid into Chinese.

His success was due to his personal qualities, his complete adaptation to Chinese customs and to his authoritative knowledge of the sciences. He is remembered for his Chinese works on religious and moral topics as well as works on scientific topics such as the *astrolobe, sphere, arithmetic, measure and isoperimeters.* For four centuries, even through times of terrible persecutions, the massive eight-foot tomb of Matteo Ricci was carefully preserved - as were tombs of the many other 17th-century Jesuit scientists who died in China. His story is told by Jonathan Spence in the 1984 best seller *The*

Memory   Palace   of   Matteo   Ricci.   The   Encyclopedia
Britannica   reports,   "Probably   no   European   name   of   past
centuries   is   so   well   known   in   China   as   that   of   Li-ma-teu
(Ricci Matteo)." (Ban, DSB, Ham, JLx, O'M, Som)

St.   Alphonsus
Rodriguez
(Italian: 1530-1617)

St.   Alphonsus

Alphonsus   was   a   Coadjutor   Brother.
He   entered   the   Society   after   the
death   of   his   wife.   He   spent   his   life
as   a   sacristan   and   porter.   During
this   time   he   had   great   influence   o n
the   young   Jesuits   of   the   house: St.
Peter   Claver's   interest   in   working
with   the   slaves   of   Cartagena   originated   from   the   influence   of   St.   Alphonsus.   Many   of   the   community,
knowing   the   Brother's   remarkable
knowledge   of   spiritual   matters,
sought   his   advice   and   direction.
After   school,   students   told   him   their   plans   for   the   future;
priests,   businessmen,   parents   came   to   seek   guidance.   Some
even   brought   their   wayward   children   to   him,   looking   to
him   for   some   suggestions.   Jesuit   superiors,   seeing   the   good
work   he   was   doing   among   the   townspeople,   were   eager   to
have   his   influence   spread   far   among   his   own   religious
community.   On   feast   he   was   often   sent   him   into   the   pulpit
in   the   dining   room   to   give   a   sermon.   All   sat   quietly   past
dinner   time   to   hear   Alphonsus   finish   his   sermon.   That   is   a
tribute   from   any   Jesuit   community   before   or   since.   Gerard
Manley   Hopkins   wrote   a   poem   to   commemorate   Alphonsus'
canonization. (Ban, Cor, Ham, Som, Tyl)

>   Yet   God   (that   hews   mountain   and   continent,
>   Earth,   all,   out;   who,   with   trickling   increment,
>   Veins   violets   and   tall   trees   makes   more   and   more)
>   Could   crowd   career   with   conquest   while   there   went
>   Those   years   and   years   by   of   world   without   event
>   That   in   Majorca   Alfonso   watched   the   door.

St. Alphonsus Rodriguez

(Spanish: 1598-1628)

Alphonsus Rodriguez

Alphonsus was one of three martyrs of River Plate along with John del Castillo and Roch Gonzalez. Alphonsus was thrilled to work with the latter, the very experienced missionary Roch Gonzalez, but this mission was not to last long, for both were to be martyred. Alphonsus was ordained in 1624 and then went to the Reductions in Paraguay along the River Plate. He and Roch Gonzalez immediately set about erecting the cross at whose base they would preach. Since the Jesuits were making noticeable progress among those Indians, the witch doctor Nezti saw that his own influence was waning and decided to kill them and prepared an ambush. On 15 November Alphonsus went into the woods to fell a tree to use as a bell pole on which to hang the chapel bell. The hired hands fell on the two priests, killed them, threw their bodies into the church and set it on fire. Alphonsus was 30 years old and had been on the mission for 15 days. (Ban, Cor, Som, Tyl)

Cristóbal Rodriguez

Cristóbal Rodriguez
(Spanish: 1521-1581)

Cristóbal was received into the Society by St. Francis Borgia when he was already a priest and theology professor. He traveled to Cairo as papal legate to the Coptic patriarch, who was apparently inclined to reconciliation with Rome. Mutual misunderstanding, lack of a common language, and other obstacles caused the mission to fail. Rodriguez later attended the Council of Trent, held the office of provincial superior, and acted as chaplain to the Christian forces at the battle of Lepanto. (Ban, JLx, O'M, Som)

John Rosenthal
(German: 1612-1665)

John taught rhetoric, philosophy and mathematics. Later he was assigned to preach in the Cathedral of Cologne where he attracted crowds to hear his sermons, and was the instrument in bringing many back to the practice of the Catholic faith. (Ham, JLx, Som)

John Rosenthal

Charles de la Rue

(French: 1643-1725)

Charles de la Rue

Charles was a distinguished Latinist, humanist, and court preacher during his 65 years in the Society. The early part of his career was spent in teaching humanities and rhetoric at the College of *Louis the Great* of Paris. Pierre Corneille paid Charles the compliment of translating into French some of his Latin poems, celebrating Louis XIV's victories over the Dutch and the Bavarians. From this period dates the beginning of Charles' work in drama. To the more strictly literary part of Charles' career belongs the extensive commentary on the major works of Virgil. The explanatory notes, rhetorical exercises, and indices were produced as an aid to the Dauphin. Charles became a court preacher and spiritual director to the nobility. He enjoyed a great reputation as a preacher, and many of his publications were funeral orations. Although immersed in court life, Charles longed to go to Canada and to labor among the North American Indians as a missionary. His superiors thought his talents were better used in France. (Ham, JLx, JLP, Som)

Alphonsus Salmerón
(Spanish: 1514-1585)

Alphonsus   Salmerón

Alphonsus   was   a   First   Companion.   Later   as   provincial   of   Naples   he   experienced   the   great   demand   for   more   Jesuit   schools   so   common   in   Europe   at   the   time,   but   he   had   to   cope   with   the   fact   that   there   were   simply   not   enough   men   to   fill   the   demand.   Pope   Paul   IV   tried   to   get   the   Jesuits   to   introduce   choir,   which   was   contrary   to   Ignatius'   plan   for   the   Society   and   clearly   contrary   to   the   Jesuit   Constitutions.   Salmerón   accompanied   the   Superior   General   Laynez   to   present   to   the   pope   this   Jesuit   position   on   choir   approved   by   the   Society's   First   General   Congregation.   The   Pontiff   addressed   them   in   very   heated   and   intemperate   terms,   accusing   Ignatius   of   being   a   tyrant   and   the   Jesuits   of   being   rebels   for   not   introducing   choir.   He   then   commanded   them   to   introduce   choir   in   all   their   houses.   They   did   so   immediately   until   the   death   of   Paul   IV   a   few   years   later.   The   succeeding   Pontiff   Pius   IV   repealed   Paul's   decree.   (Ban, Ham, JLx, O'M, Som)

John   Salvatierra
(Italian: 1648-1717)

John   Salvatierra

John   was   one   of   the   m a n y
Jesuits   inspired   by   the   Jesuit
explorer   Eusebio   Kino,   S.J.
The   intelligent   and   c o u r a -
geous   Juan   Salvatierra   labored   in   Lower   California,   a n
arid   land   and   dangerous   e n -
vironment.   From   the   time   o f
his   arrival   there   until   h i s
death   20 years   later   he   s u c -
ceeded   in   building   a   s t r i n g
of   missions   through-out   t h e
peninsula.   It   is   a   m o n u m e n t
to   his   refusal   to   be   overwhelmed   by   the   man's   opposition
and   nature's   inhospitality.   The   number   of   Jesuit   m a r t y r s
was   increased   by   the   indigenous   natives   who   were   slow   i n
understanding   what   John   Salvatierra   and   the   other   5 5
Jesuits   were   trying   to   do   for   them   in   California.   (Ban,   Ham,
JLx,   Som)

Noel   Sanadon
(French: 1676-1733)

Noel Sanadon

Noel was a Latin poet and taught humanities at Caen and at the *Louis the Great* College. Noel went to Tours where he functioned as a prefect of studies and there finished his translation and edition of Horace's Odes and Epodes. The edition caused quite a stir at the time since Noel drastically altered the arrangement of the poems. His French translations of the poems were used extensively for a long period of time. Noel also published a collection of his own poetry under the title *Carminum   libri*. (Ham, JLx, JLP, Som)

An extra glimpse of the early Society

At a conservative estimate there were between the years 1650 and 1700 about 500 continental Jesuit colleges, which "had a vast international chain of the same number of playhouses, engaged in a coordinated production of plays." There were at least two plays a year in each college, in addition to those presented on special occasions, such as the visits of royalty. It has been estimated that at least 100,000 plays were produced on these Jesuit stages in this period. It is impossible to include a comprehensive account of this massive development in a short article, but the nearest approach to this task is contained in the study by W. H. McCabe, S.J. (*Catholic Encyclopedia*, 1967, **7**, p.893)

Thomas Sanchez

(Spanish: 1550-1610)

Thomas Sanchez

Thomas taught moral theology and the weight of his authority on moral questions was quite impressive. He won wide recognition particularly for his frequently re-edited 1602 book *The Holy Sacrament of Matrimony.* Thomas Sanchez expressed himself with clarity and precision, especially regarding distinctions needed regarding the principle of Probabilism. For example he stated that a genuine probable opinion required that "it does not rest on superficial grounds; the view of a wise and learned man is, however, not a superficial but, rather, a material ground." (Ban, Ham, JLx, Som)

Matthew Sarbiewski
(Polish: 1593-1640)

Matthew has been called the "Christian Horace" due to his poetic skill, his emotional power and the richness of his language. His Latin poems awakened memories of the cadences of Rome's finest poetry. The great number of editions and translations of his poetry into virtually all the European languages emphatically confirms the tremendous popularity his works have enjoyed over the past three centuries. (Ban, Ham, JLx, JLP, Som)

Matthew   Sarbiewski

An extra glimpse of the early Society

Music was taught in the Jesuit schools from the beginning, especially in Jesuit theater, so that by the end of the 16th century there had developed a noteworthy musical life in some of the Jesuit colleges. In his book *Jesuits and Music,* Thomas Culley, S.J. reports that music was quite important at many Jesuit colleges. In spite of the fact that music was cultivated very early by the Jesuits, Culley comments: "It is a pity that so much musical activity has thus far interested so few historians of music."

Bl. William Saultemouche

(French: 1555-1593)

William   Saultemouche

William was a Coadjutor Brother of exceptional de-votion and humility. Pres-ent at heated theological debates between his com-panion Bl. James Salès and the Calvinist ministers, William declared: "I will die with you for the truth of your arguments." He was martyred along with James whose preaching strengthened the Catholics around Aubenas, France. James' writings and ser-mons concerning the Eucharist marked him for death by his enemies, the Huguenots, who were obsessed with hatred for the Catholic doctrine of the Eucharist. On 5 February Huguenot troops struck the town of Aubenas and imposed their own rule on this formerly Catholic town. James and William came for one of their many public appearances in the local square and were confronted by Huguenot ministers. A debate on the Eucharist followed in which James spoke eloquently enough to sway those listening. This worried the Huguenot leader, so both James and William were arrested, thrown into prison and the next day executed in the town square. (Ban, Ham, JLx, Som, Tyl)

John Schall von Bell
(German: 1591-1669)

John was a missionaryand astronomer in China. During a change of rulers John was imprisoned and condemned to a slow death, but an earthquake intervened and he was released. His *Trigonometria* and his many other scientific works were written and published in China. John constructed a double stellar hemisphere to illustrate planetary movement and wrote 150 treatises in Chinese concerning the calendar. His tomb as well as those of the Jesuits Ricci and

John Schall von Bell

Verbiest was restored after the Cultural Revolution and relocated on the grounds of a Communist training school where these tombs can still be visited today.(Ban, DSB, Ham, JLx, Som)

Adam discussing astronmy with China's emperor

Christopher Scheiner
(German: 1575-1650)

Christopher   Scheiner

Christopher was a brilliant geometer, physicist and astronomer. He published many scientific works. During his long controversy with Kepler, he adopted the pseudonym "Appelles," the mythological figure who could draw the finest line. He engaged Galileo in controversy, and many of his publications deal with aspects of their discussions on the systems of the universe. He discovered sunspots independently of Galileo and explained the elliptical form of the sun near the horizon as the effect of refraction. In his *Oculus* (1619) he showed that the retina is the seat of vision. His invention (1631) for magnifying curves and maps, the pantograph, is an early example of a geometric transformation and can still be purchased in stationery stores.

Scheiner trained young mathematicians and organized public debates on current events in astronomy, such as the heliocentric vs. the geocentric theories of the universe. In his major work, *Rosa Ursina sive sol* (1630), he confirmed his findings and method and gave his measurement of the inclination of the axis of rotation of the sunspots to the plane of the ecliptic, a measurement which is off only a few minutes from the true value. Scheiner explained the elliptical shape of the sun near the horizon as the effect of refraction, a phenomenon discovered by another Jesuit named Grimaldi. He gave one of his telescopes to the archduke of Tyrol who was more interested in the scenery than in stars and complained that the image was inverted. Scheiner inserted another lens to invert the image again and so created one of the first terrestrial telescopes. (Ban, DSB, JLx, Som)

Andrew   Schott
(Belgian: 1552-1629)

Andrew taught rhetoric at Louvain before entering the Society and afterwards in Rome. His presentations in class were well known for their remarkable erudition and precise criticism of the author being studied. He had many publications. (Ban, Ham, Som)

Andrew   Schott

**Stamp of a painting
by Daniel Seghers**

Daniel Seghers
(Belgian: 1590-1661)

Daniel Seghers

Daniel was an artist famous for his floral designs. Daniel did not paint portraits. Rather, the animals, humans, buildings etc. enclosed in his floral frame were painted by other artists such as Peter Paul Rubens who frequently visited Daniel to admire his paintings. In fact Rubens liked the opportunity to paint the figures necessary to finish Daniel's pictures. Few artists have had as many imitators as Daniel. It is surprising to find this quiet Jesuit Coadjutor Brother so influential in bureaucratic circles. Kings and Queens used their influence to get his paintings into their collections. At one time the famous diplomat and physicist, Constantine Huygens, used his friendship with Daniel to have a painting commissioned for the Prince of Orange. Later Daniel was asked to produce a fitting painting for Emperor Ferdinand III to present to Queen Christina of Sweden in order to accelerate the end of the Thirty Year War. Her generals feared her because she had a keener mind than any general or diplomat, but the ardent art collector Christina was calmed by a Segher painting. Later she visited the Jesuits many times and, on Christmas night, 1654, at Brussels, she made a private profession of the Catholic Faith.

About 200 paintings by Daniel Seghers have survived for 300 years and are scattered all around the world. (Ham, JLx, Som)

Paul Segneri
(Italian: 1624-1694)

Paul Segneri

Paul was a preacher and retreat giver and made a powerful spiritual impact on the Italian people whom he directed. For 27 years Paul traveled throughout Tuscany and the Papal States. He has been called the John Wesley of the seventeenth century, speaking with the eloquence of St. Bernadine of Siena. He walked 800 miles a year and attracted as many as 20,000 while giving a mission. Once he came to Rome as the papal preacher for the Lenten season. He had extended meetings with Pope Innocent, and, with simple candor, he tried to persuade his Jesuit Superior General, Tirso González, to abandon his position (and withdraw his book) condemning the doctrine of *Probabilism*. He pointed out that a Superior General's obligation was to rule, not to write books. He quoted the many authorities in moral theology who favored the doctrine of Probabilism. Paul, however, did not succeed in convincing Tirso González. (Ban, Ham, JLx, Som)

Jacques   Sirmond
(French: 1559-1651)

Jacques   Sirmond

Jacques exposed quite convincingly the Calvinistic basis of Jansenism in his critique of Bishop Cornelius Jansen's *Augustinus.* Jacques was a prominent scholar, with a sense of history, a deep respect for facts whose erudition gave a new direction to theological studies. Jacques did prodigious work in editing texts, many of which have become widely used editions of the Greek and Latin Fathers of the Church. He also was one of the highly respected Jesuits who helped solve an impasse between King Henry VI and Pope Clement VIII by requesting that the pope lift a decree of excommunication against Henry. (Ban, Ham, JLx, Som)

Peter   Skarga
(Polish: 1536-1612)

This popular theologian, apologist and preacher was called the "Polish Bossuet", due to his oratorical abilities. He abandoned theology for preaching; he also abandoned literary activities for the sake of spreading Catholicism. He established charitable societies in many Polish cities to care for the sick, to guide and protect young women, to clothe the poor and to shield the uneducated from

Peter   Skarga

usurers. Peter also founded and enlarged Jesuit schools in Poland. (Ban, Ham, JLx, Som)

St. Robert Southwell
(English: 1561-1595)

Death of Robert Southwell

Robert was a Jesuit poet. He was hanged, drawn and quartered at Tyburn for preaching the Catholic Faith in Queen Elizabeth's England. He belongs to that band of Jesuit English martyrs during the persecution of Catholics from 1535 to 1681 who were determined not to abandon the Catholic laity, but to be with them, providing the consolation of the Eucharist. Robert's father had conformed to the new Protestant religion. Robert joined the Jesuits in 1578 and after ordination left Rome for England with Henry Garnet. Both were almost arrested upon landing but escaped capture and went on to work with the Catholics in London. Robert's writings were extremely popular with his contemporaries such as Ben Johnson who declared that he wished he had written some of Robert's poems. The best known of his poems are *The Burning Babe* and *Saint Peter's Complaint* (1595), in which he made experiments with verse that were further developed by other poets, including Shakespeare. Robert spent six years in zealous and successful missionary work and moved under various disguises traveling from one Catholic house to another. Finally he was betrayed in 1592. Robert never gave any information about other priests or Catholics, even though for three years he was interrogated under atrocious torture. He was transferred to Newgate prison where he was confined in a dungeon swarming with vermin and frequently chained in such a way that he could neither stand, sit nor lie down. His jailers were exasperated at his answers. When asked his age he would reply: "near that of our Blessed Savior." The execution of this young talented poet shocked the court and the whole country. (Ban, JLx, Som, Tyl)

Frederick Spe von Langenfeld
(German: 1595-1635)

Frederick Spe von Langenfeld

Frederick wrote hymns which are still found in hymnals, both Catholic and Lutheran. He is considered one of the most important poets of the Baroque period because of his hymns found in his two books *Trutz-Nachtigal* and *Goldenes Tugenbuch* (a book much loved by Leibniz). During his seminary days he taught children catechism by using hymns of his own. He authored the book *Cautio Criminalis* which protested the detestable witch trials common in his time, and especially common during the Thirty Years War, trials that came about because of Luther's fixation on the influence of devils. (Canisius' famous Catechism omitted all mention of devils.) The thesis of the book was simply that witches did not exist, and that innocent women had no way of proving their innocence. His conclusion was a novel one: people are innocent until proven guilty. One of his assignments was to administer to the condemned "witches" in their last hours. About them he wrote: "I have not been able to find anything but innocence everywhere . . . and have concluded that innocent people are falsely considered culpable." Although his book eventually brought about reforms, the initial reaction of both ecclesiastical and secular authorities was that his book as well as his crusade were dangerous. An attempt was made on his life leaving him with head wounds and pain that stayed with him for the rest of his life. In 1635, while caring for victims of a plague he caught the plague, and "died a death which was comparable to martyrdom." (Ban, JLx, Som)

Bl. Charles Spinola
(Italian: 1564-1622)

Charles Spinola

Charles was a missionary to China who died a martyr's death during the Great Martyrdom of Nagasaki on 10 September, 1622. His companion was Bl. Sebastian Kimura, S.J., the first Japanese to be ordained and the cousin of Bl. Leonard Kimura, mentioned earlier. Around this time 87 Jesuits were martyred after enduring imprisonment and terrible torture. Charles had entered Japan to assist the Christians during this frightful "Great Persecution under emperor Iycyasu. He eluded priest hunters for three years but was finally captured and brought to a prison near Nagasaki. Charles called his pen similar to a bird cage since it was an enclosure made of stakes with neither walls nor roof, open to the heat of the sun, cold rain, icy snow, and whipping winds. They were fed a few handfuls of rice daily and the stench was intolerable. It was so crowded that the prisoners had to squat and lean upon each other. The Christians in Nagasaki bribed some of the guards to supply them with all that was needed for saying Mass, so that Charles celebrated Mass every day for his fellow prisoners. After four years of this Charles was taken to Nagasaki and put to death by slow fire. (Ban, Ham, JLx, Som, Tyl)

Commemorative stamp of Frederick Spe von Langenfeld

Joseph   Stepling
(Czechoslovakian: 1716-1778)

Joseph   Stepling

At the age of 17 Joseph calcu-
lated with great accuracy the
1733 lunar eclipse. Later Euler
was among his long list of
correspondents.   He trans-
posed Aristotelian logic into
formulas, thus becoming a n
early precursor of modern
logic. Even though he passed
up a professorship in philosophy in favor of a chair i n
mathematics, Empress Maria
Theresa appointed him director of the faculty of philosophy at Prague as part of the
reform of higher education.
He was very interested i n
cultivating the exact sciences and founded a society for the
study of science modeled on the Royal Society of London.
Many of the findings of the this society were published. At
his death Maria Theresa ordered a monument to be erected
in his honor in the library at the University of Prague.
(Ban, Ham, JLx, Som)

Francis   Suarez

(Spanish: 1548-1617)

Francis   Suarez

Francis was one of the great Spanish theologians, considered supreme among the Jesuit thinkers of his time. He possessed a tremendous breadth of intellectual interest and was unusually insightful when dealing with speculative problems. His entire work runs to 23 volumes. Francis was one of 4,000 Jesuits who volunteered to serve on the China mission.

Francis unintentionally caused an eruption of feeling against French Jesuits with his publication of his Defense of the Catholic Faith meant to contest England's Oath of Allegiance. The book offended the sensibilities of the royalists and a new storm broke over the Society in France, Parliament ordered the volume to be burned and the French Provincial requested the Italian and Spanish provincials: "I hope that you will put an absolute ban in your provinces on the publication in the future of any. similar book." Francis tried to unravel some of the speculative moral and legal problems that came with colonialization and thus attempted a systematic articulation of international law for what was emerging as a community of nations. He is considered one of the main sources of the impetus for independence in South America. In Francis historians discern the creator of the intellectual framework for independence. His doctrine on civil authority, affirming that government receives its authority from God indirectly through the mediation of the people, disposed the educated classes for the break with an autocratic crown. In the late eighteenth century, Spain certainly showed its fear of this teaching and banned Francis' offending volumes. (Ban, Ham, JLx, O'M, Som)

John Suffren
(French: 1565-1641)

John was confessor for Marie de Medici. When he was made confessor to King Louis XIII by the Minister of State, Richelieu with the admonition "Do not go near the king unless summoned", he remarked: "I shall not be long in this position." When John made it clear that the Jesuits would not deny the pope's indirect temporal power, he was removed by Richelieu. (Ban, Ham, JLx, Som)

John Suffren

Michael Tamburini

Michael Tamburini
(Italian: 1648-1730)

Michael was the fourteenth Superior General of the Society, and no general since St. Ignatius faced such persistent and troublesome attacks on the Society. During his 24-year term he experienced a concerted campaign of slander and vilification against the Society. An early attack concerned the Chinese Rites Decree. Europe had been fascinated by the efforts of the Jesuits to accommodate the gestures and vestments of Catholic ritual to a vaguely Confucian ceremonial. The group opposed to this effort at adaptation consisted of a monolithic Roman Curia abetted by Dominicans and Franciscans and also by Pascal's Jansenists - who in fact desired nothing less than the complete dissolution of the Society. The Jesuits were convinced that Christianity can be reconciled with a culture fundamentally different from the one in which it had evolved, but their plan was condemned. The Roman decision was influenced by Roman politics and has been called *suicidal* for Christianity in Asia. The onus of arguing the Jesuit position in the face of growing political pressure on the pope fell to Michael Tamburini. Actually, he had to present the Jesuit case before two popes, Pope Innocent XIII and Benedict XIII. The papal legate to China, Carlo Mezzabarba, had assured the Jesuits their practices merited only the highest praise, but when Carlo returned to Rome he joined the loud chorus condemning the Society. The Congregation for the Propagation of the Faith wanted a complete condemnation of the Society which would prohibit novices from entering and reduce vows to three years, so that the Society would soon cease to exist. This was an omen for the future since it happened fifty years before the Suppression in 1773. Pope Benedict XIII was convinced by Michael Tamburini's presentation and did not suppress the Society but did issue an edict condemning the Jesuit practices in China. Benedict advised the missionaries that conversions were due to God's grace, urged them to preach the Faith in its purity, encouraged the Jesuits to martyrdom, and commanded that they take an oath of obedience regarding the Chinese rites. The Jesuits were certainly martyred in great numbers and under terrible conditions, but in the meantime the Church in Rome squandered a magnificent and successful missionary endeavor. (Ban, Ham, JLx, Som)

Bl. Balthazar Torres

(Spanish: 1563-1626)

Balthazar Torres

Balthazar was one of the 87 martyrs during the great persecution in Nagasaki. Balthasar was sent to Goa, India, then, after his ordination, taught theology in the seminary there. He was sent to Japan in 1600 and spent the next 25 years working with Japanese Christians. Rather than leave the country when the expulsion edict of 1614 was published, Balthasar went into hiding and secretly continued his apostolic ministry until he was captured in 1626 in a small village near Nagasaki. With him was his catechist, Michael Tozo, and both were sent to prison in Omura. Balthasar died with seven other Jesuit martyrs in Nagasaki on 20 June 1626. (Ham, JLx, Som, Tyl)

Anthony Turner

(English: 1628-1679)

Anthony Turner

Anthony was the son of a Protestant minister who became enraged when his wife and two sons, puzzled by the number of different Protestant sects, sought information about Catholicism and showed that they were interested in becoming Catholics. Anthony with his brother Edward, converted to Catholicism, joined the Jesuits and worked among the English Catholics. Both died martyrs in England: Edward in prison, Anthony hanged at Tyburn with four other Jesuits. Before he was hanged, drawn and quartered Anthony told the surrounding crowd: " I am bound in conscience to do myself that justice as to declare upon oath my innocence from the horrid crime of treason with which I am falsely accused. I am as free from the treason I am accused of as a child that is just born. I die a Roman Catholic and humbly beg the prayers of such for my happy passage into a better life." (Ban, Bas, Ham, Tyl)

Alessandro Valignano

(Italian: 1538-1606)

Alessandro Valignano

Alessandro was the man who consolidated the missionary efforts of the Jesuits in India, Japan and China which Xavier had started. He labored there for 33 years. He convinced Pope Gregory XIII to make the mission to Japan an exclusively Jesuit mission on the grounds that the distinct Franciscan religious garb as well as their unusual methods would create the impression that Catholicism was just as fragmented as Buddhism and unworthy of investigation. When the Franciscans did come 23 years later they proved Alessandro correct when they created a disedifying split in the apostolate because their approach was so different from the Jesuits. They looked with contempt on the Japanese culture which the Jesuits greatly admired. The Jesuits were much more cautious in distributing pious items such as rosaries which might lead to superstition while the Franciscans condemned the intellectual approach of the Jesuits. Alessandro's greatest fear was fulfilled and these Spanish Franciscans were seen as a fifth column preparing for a Spanish assault. This led to the great persecution of 1597 which resulted in 26 martyrs, including both Franciscans and Jesuits. During all this time communication with Rome was extremely slow. A 1589 letter of Alessandro arrived in Rome 17 years later in 1607. Without Roman instructions Alessandro knew how to use his vast authority and he built seminaries, reorganized the mission and started the first movable press in Japan. He insisted on accommodating to Japanese dress, food and housing and ordered intense Japanese language studies. To finance these changes he received permission from the pope to invest in silk trade with Macao. It was Alessandro who was the historical model for the Jesuit Visitor in the apocryphal story *Shogun*.

Alessandro aimed not just at making Christians in Japan but at making Japan Christian. While he constantly counseled caution and prudence, at the same time his strategy was always to cultivate and if possible convert the powerful and the prominent, and then to use their power, fame and influence to promote Christianity. He considered the employment of these secular means to sacred ends legitimate and necessary, but it was a dangerous strategy and became more dangerous as the successive lords, all of them intolerant of any power, fame or influence other than their own, came progressively closer to omnipotence. The persecutions continued for more than two and a half centuries. The only Christian communities to survive them were the 'hidden Christians', and their survival was their own astonishing achievement, for there were no *Christian samurai* to lead them. Alessandro's motto was "Pray to God, sailor, but row for the shore." and he was exasperated at inaction on the part of local superiors. Also, it was Alessandro more than anyone else, who taught the missionaries that becoming a follower of Christ does not mean becoming a European or ceasing to be Japanese. In 1614 Diego de Mesquita wrote of the Christians of Japan: "There does not seem to be any Church in the whole of Christendom which surpasses them. Indeed, I regard them as the best in the world. They are a noble and rational people all of whom are very much subject to reason, and when they become Christians and begin to go to confession they live very well, taking great care of their souls, and anxious to keep our holy law, and with a great desire for salvation, correcting the vices they had when they were pagans." More can be read about this remarkable man, Alessandro Valignano, in *Valignano's Mission Principles for Japan* by Josef Franz Schütte. (Ban, Ham, JLx, O'M, Som)

Gabriel   Vasquez
(Spanish: 1551-1604)

Gabriel Vasquez

Gabriel   was   one   of   the   great
Catholic theologians. He taught at
the Roman College where he insisted on precise thought and lucid expression. He enlivened dis-
putations   by   his   vast   erudition,
quick   intelligence,   and   lively
language.   The   contemporary
theological   world   linked   the two
names, Suarez and Vasquez. Energetic and persistent in his manner, Vasquez always maintained
an independence   of   thought   in
his   search   for   truth. Two popes, Benedict XIV and Leo XIII,
who   appreciated   intellectual   achievement,   paid special
tribute to his scholarly endowments. Gabriel was the first
among   the   Jesuits   to   teach   Probabilism   which   spread
quickly   among   Jesuit   theologians;   they   later   became   its
most ardent defenders. (Ban, Ham, JLx, Som)

An extra glimpse of the early Society

Ohms Law $V = IR$ commemorates three of the worlds most familiar names,
Ohm, Volt and Ampere whose symbols are stamped on   all   electrical
instruments. These three men were connected with Jesuit schools.   George Ohm
taught physics in the Jesuit college in Cologne. André Ampère sponsored the
education of the abandoned students of Jesuit schools who, during the *Terror* of
1830, were dismissed by the French Government when it expelled the Jesuits
from France and then confiscated their schools. Alessandro Volta joined the
Jesuits for a short time (as did his father) and then interacted with Jesuit
scientists for the rest his life. He developed and built the first electric battery.

S. G. Horace Vecchi

(French: 1577-1612)

Martyrdom of Horace Vecchi

Horace was martyred in Chile. He had worked among the natives in the settlements the Jesuits founded to protect them from slave traders and from the raids of enemy tribes. He himself was killed during such a raid. After his theology training and ordination in Peru, his missionary apostolate in Chile lasted only four years. Horace was killed by the Araucanian tribe in Chile who had continually menaced the Christians there. The reason for the tribe's hatred was partly because three wives of one of their chiefs had escaped and become Christians. When the wives were not returned, the Spanish soldiers were afraid to enter Araucanian territory. The Jesuit Provincial, however, thought differently and sent three Jesuits into the territory to convert the tribe. Five days after they arrived, the offended chief came and demanded his wives. When the missionaries refused on the grounds that the now Christian women did not belong to him, they were killed and became the first martyrs of Chile. (Ham, JLx, Som, Tyl)

Ferdinand Verbiest
(Belgian: 1623-1688)

Ferdinand   Verbiest

Ferdinand was a geometer, astronomer and missionary to China. His Chinese name was Nan Huai-Jen and he is listed as one of the 108 heroes of the popular novel Shui Hu Chuan. Having taught the Emperor geometry, science, art and literature, he became a frequent guest of the royal household. The Emperor brought him on many expeditions and entrusted him with a number of important projects of the empire. He wrote many religious, as well as a large number of astronomical and mathematical, works in the Manchu language. His funeral was a stately affair accompanied by bands, standard bearers, portraits of himself and the saints, 50 horsemen and representatives from the Emperor. His tomb in Beijing, alongside the other two giants of the China mission, Matteo Ricci and Adam Schall, was restored after the cultural revolution and can be visited today. He restructured the calendar, determined the elusive Russo-Chinese border and rebuilt and directed the Imperial Observatory, still a Beijing tourist attraction. (Ban, DSB, Ham, JLx, Som)

Stamp of Ferdinand

Anthony   Verjus
(French: 1632-1706)

Anthony   Verjus

Anthony was a procurator for the Jesuit mission in the Middle East. He was a frequent correspondent of Leibniz who considered religious orders such as the Society "a heavenly host upon earth . . . Whosoever ignores or despises this has but a poor and debased conception of virtue."   Leibniz   was   on friendly   terms   and regularly corresponded with a number of Jesuits such as Anthony, perhaps because of Anthony's connections with Jesuit Foreign Missions. On several occasions, Leibniz defended Jesuits, stating that "he wishes to be regarded as a 'warm friend' of the Jesuits" and he followed with considerable interest Jesuit missionary work, the scientific importance of which he fully appreciated. Leibniz once drew up a memorandum in which he expatiated on the merits of the Jesuit missionaries. (Ham, JLx, Som)

Anthony   Vieira
(Portuguese: 1608-1697)

Anthony   Vieira

Anthony   was   a   famous preacher   and   has   been called   *Portugal's   Amazing Polymath*. One   of   the   classical   writers   of   Portuguese prose,   Vieira   was   made   court orator   and   adviser   to   the King.   Not   always   tactful, however,   he   was   a   staunch defender   of   the   "New   Christians"   (Jewish   converts),   and so   he   won   the   enmity   of   the Inquisition;   he   was   reviled for   his   defense   of   the   Jews and   he   claimed   that   *the   Dominicans   live   off   the   faith while   the   Jesuits   die   for   the   faith*. Antonio's   powerful preaching   gained   him   considerable   influence   over   John IV   and   the   Portuguese   court.   He   urged   the   Portuguese   to bathe   their   "swords   in   the   blood   of   heretics   in   Europe,   in the   blood   of   Muslims   in   Africa,   in   the   blood   of   heathen   in Asia   and   in   America   so   that   all   may   be   placed   gloriously beneath   the   feet   of   the   successor   of   St.   Peter".

The   Jesuit   General   Carafa,   uneasy - with   his   activities, decided   that   he   should   leave   the   Society,   while   King   John IV   offered   him   a   Bishopric.   Vieira,   however,   fooled   them both   and   insisted   on   staying   in   the   Society.   King   John   who considered   Vieira   *o   primeiro   homen   do   mundo*   blocked Carafa's   plan   to   expel   him.   Although   Vieira   did   not   leave the   Society,   he   did   leave   Lisbon's   court   and   went   to   Brazil where   he   founded   missions   among   the   Maranhao   and Amazon   Indians.   In   Brazil   he   occasionally   represented King   John   IV   on   diplomatic   missions.   He   labored   among these   Indians   and   alienated   the   colonialists   by   his   bitter denunciation   of   the   European   slave   traders.   At   his   funeral slaves   and   the   poor   were   his   chief   mourners.   Today   the Jesuit   school   in   Bahia   is   named   in   his   honor.   (Ban,   Ham, JLx,   Som)

Gregory St. Vincent

(Belgian: 1584-1667)

Gregory St. Vincent

Gregory studied mathematics under Christopher Clavius. Gregory was a brilliant mathematician and is looked upon as one of the founders of analytical geometry. He established a famous school of mathematics at Antwerp. Gregory deals with conics, surfaces and solids from a new point of view, employing infinitesimals in a way differing from Cavalieri. Gregory was probably the first to use the word *exhaurire* in a geometrical sense. From this word arose the name of "method of exhaustion," as applied to the method of Euclid and Archimedes. Gregory used a method of transformation of one conic into another, called *per subtendas* (by chords), which contains germs of analytic geometry. He created another special slicing method which was used in the study of solids. Unlike Archimedes, who kept on dividing distances only until a certain degree of smallness was reached, Gregory permitted the subdivisions to continue *ad infinitum* and obtained a geometric series that was infinite. Gregory was the first to apply geometric series to the "Achilles" problem of Zeno (in which the tortoise always wins the race with the swift Achilles since he has an unbeatable head start) and to look upon the paradox as a question in the summation of an infinite series. Moreover, Gregory was the first to state the exact time and place of overtaking the tortoise. He spoke of the limit as an obstacle against further advance, similar to a rigid wall. Apparently, he was not troubled by the fact that in his theory the variable does not reach its limit. His exposition of the "Achilles" paradox was favorably received by Leibniz and by other geometers over a century later. (DSB, Ham, JLx, Som)

Ignazio   Visconti
(Italian: 1682-1755)

Ignazio   Visconti

Ignazio   served   as   the   16th   Superior   General.   He   encouraged
the   humanities   in   Jesuit
schools   and   suggested   that
each   teacher   be   provided   with
a   copy   of   *For   Christian   Teachers   of   Literature.   A   Way   to
Learn   and   Instruct*   (1691),
written   in   Latin   by   one   of   the
most   articulate   Jesuit   advocates   of   the   classical   languages,   Joseph   de   Jouvancy.
Ignazio   died   after   only   four
years   in   office.   (Ban,   Ham,   JLx,
Som)

An extra glimpse of the early Society

Giovanni Lorenzo Bernini had many Jesuit friends and he took his Catholic faith
very seriously. Once he had made the *Spiritual Exercises* he committed his life
to Ignatian principles and felt missioned to use his enormous talent to highlight
the beauties of God's creation, to make tangible the lessons of the *Exercises* and
to help people find God in their lives. Commentators on his life emphasize how
habitually focused he was on the *Spiritual Exercises*.   It was not merely that he
prayed daily in the Jesuit *Gesù Church* in Rome but also that his art reflected
the centrality of God, the Gospel and the *Spiritual Exercises* in his own life.

Joseph   Walcher
(Austria: 1719-1803)

Joseph   Walcher

Joseph was a mathemati-
cian and taught mechanics
and hydraulics at the College of Thérésien at the
University of Vienna for
17 years. He was also an
engineer who is credited
with saving the country-
side from floods by using
the dikes at Lake Rofner-
Lise. After the Suppression
he was named the director
of navigation along the
Danube and director
general of public buildings
in Vienna. His 50th anniversary of ordination was
commemorated in a magnificent public ceremony by the
city. (Ban, Ham, Som)

Henry Walpole

St. Henry Walpole
(English: 1558-1595)

Henry found his vocation in an unusual manner while present at the death of Edmund Campion. As the executioners were quartering Edmund some blood spattered on Henry's clothing which he took to be a call from God to follow in Edmund's footsteps. Henry left his law studies, entered the Jesuits at St. Andrew's Novitiate in Rome, was ordained in Paris and was arrested the day after coming to the English Mission. He proclaimed that he had come to England "to convert the English to God". Brought to the Tower of London he was cruelly tortured no less than 14 times upon the rack, losing the use of his fingers. Henry was afterwards brought to York, there tried for high treason for his priesthood and then suffered the same brutal death imposed on Edmund Campion: hanged, drawn and quartered. (Ban, Bas, JLx, Som, Tyl)

Emblem for the canonization of the 40 English martyrs in October, 1970: Henry Walpole was included in the 40.

Stanislaus Warszewicki

(Polish: 1530-1591)

Stanislaus   Warszewicki

Stanislaus was sent as a papal envoy to Stockholm in 1574 when King John III of Sweden showed interest in becoming Catholic, in converting his people and in joining Sweden to Catholic political alliances. Stanislaus was able to initiate discussions with the king so that two months later, John III had become so convinced that he declared his readiness to introduce the Catholic liturgy into the Swedish Church. Stanislaus appealed to his superiors for a Jesuit who knew the Swedish language. Rome sent an intelligent and creative Norwegian, Laurits Nielssen (Laurentius Norvegus) with whom King John held public debates in order to move his people toward Catholicism. Laurits delivered such convincing lectures on Lutheranism and Catholicism that the king made Laurits a theology professor at the newly founded seminary in Stockholm, and urged all Protestant priests to attend his lectures. By the spring of 1579 Laurits had 70 students registered, including 30 Lutheran ministers. Then it was clear that the time had come for Rome to enter a new stage in the negotiations, so Stanislaus was replaced by Antonio Possevino whose disappointing story is told under his name. This promising Swedish enterprise came very close to succeeding but failed because of a fatal Roman decision which was insensitive to the attitudes of the Swedish Protestants and the precarious position of King John. After five years spent in the mission to Sweden, Stanislaus was sent to Lithuania where his eloquence, wisdom and sincerity brought many back to the Catholic Faith. He died while helping the victims of the 1591 plague. (DSB, Ham, JLx, Som)

Thomas Whitbread

(English: 1618-1679)

Thomas was an English martyr who died during the Titus Oates Plot. He had used the alias *Harcourt*. Thomas became provincial of all the English Jesuits and made a tour of the seminaries on the Continent. At the college of St. Omer he met Titus Oates who had once been an Anglican minister but had been defrocked because of his irregular life. He then

Thomas Whitbread

converted to Catholicism, attended the Jesuit colleges in Spain, and had been expelled from both of them. He applied to enter the Society but was rejected by Thomas Whitbread. Oates sought revenge against the Jesuits and concocted a detailed plot in which the Jesuits were supposed to have planned the assassination of the king and the re-establishment of the Catholic Church. Eventually Thomas was arrested with two other Jesuits, Thomas Fenwick and William Ireland and brought to trial. The jailers were concerned about one of Fenwick's legs; because the chain was so tight, they thought they would have to amputate; they abandoned the idea since conviction was certain at the trial. Titus Oates was the principal witness at the trial. Five Jesuits were found guilty and brought to execution at Tyburn. Before being hanged, Thomas Whitbread said "I do declare to you here present and to the whole world, that I go out of the world as innocent and as free from any guilt of these things laid to my charge in this matter, as I came into the world from my mother's womb. As for those who have most falsely accused me I do heartily forgive them, and beg of God to grant them His holy grace, that they may repent of their unjust proceedings against me." Suddenly a rider came with a message announcing that the king was granting the five priests their lives on the condition that they acknowledge their part in the plot and reveal all then knew about it. The martyrs thanked the king for his inclination to mercy but since there was no plot, they could not acknowledge guilt. Then they were hanged, drawn and quartered. (Ban, Bas, Ham, Tyl)

Cornelius Wishaven
(Belgian: 1509-1559)

Cornelius Wishaven

Cornelius was one of the earliest Jesuits and was quite involved in many pioneering ventures. Among his precedent-setting experiences was the practice of working in a hospital during his noviceship (under Ignatius' direction), teaching in a school for non-Jesuits and in directing the first Jesuit novitiate. In 1550 this novitiate opened in Messina for ten novices, and was the start of Jesuit novices living apart from other Jesuits and also the beginning of a two year novitiate instead a single year. Having been ordained before entering the Society, Cornelius had occasion to perform exorcisms. At this time exorcisms were not unusual for Jesuits to perform, mainly because of the alternative. Jesuits did not want possession to become a matter for the Inquisition. Also they were careful to distinguish between ordinary psychological stress (for example depression would be helped simply by conversation) and much more serious behavior. (Ban, Ham, JLx, O'M, Som)

Bl. Peter Wright

(English: 1603-1651)

Peter Wright

Peter for 10 years worked as a clerk in a lawyer's office. His father had died and he had to help support his 11 siblings. Eventually he enlisted in the English army in Holland, but offended at the licentiousness of the life, he quickly left it, and was admitted to the Society in 1629. Being sent to the English Mission in 1643 he served for only a few years before he was seized by the priest hunters, committed to Newgate prison, tried for high treason and condemned to death. He was hanged at Tyburn in the presence of more than 20,000 spectators. He said to them: "This is a short passage to eternity. I was brought here charged with no other crime but being a priest. This is the cause for which I die; for this alone am I condemned and for propagating the Catholic faith. For this cause I willingly sacrifice my life, and would die a thousand times for the same, if it were necessary." He then asked the people to join him in prayer and to pray for him, concluding with "when I shall come to heaven I will do as much for you." His many friends were permitted a take his butchered body away for proper burial. (Bas, JLx, Tyl)

St. Francis Xavier

(Basque: 1506-1552)

Francis Xavier

Francis was a missionary in India, the East Indies, and Japan. Since the time of the Apostles there has not been a greater missionary. His ambitions to become a university professor were put aside when he met another Basque, Ignatius Loyola, who convinced him that the best way to use his talents was to spread the Gospel. Xavier became one of Ignatius' first companions in a fellowship that later became the *Society of Jesus*. He was the first Jesuit missionary. The story of his journeys is an epic of adventure that found him dining with head hunters, washing sores of lepers in Venice, teaching catechism to Indian children, baptizing 10,000 in a single month. He could put up with the most appalling conditions on his long sea voyages and endure the most agonizing extremes of heat and cold. Wherever he went he would seek out and help the poor and forgotten. Because of the slave trade he scolded his patron King John of Portugal: "You have no right to spread the Catholic faith while you take away all the country's riches. It upsets me to know that at the hour of your death you may be ordered out of paradise."

In a ten-year span he traveled thousands of miles - most of it on his own bare feet. He saw the greater part of the Far East. He died in 1552 on a lonely island, Sancian, near the China coast, while trying to reach mainland China. An astonishing feat! But what is especially remarkable is the fact that he left behind him a flourishing church wherever he went. Many miracles were attributed to him, but the real miracle of his life was the miracle of his personality, by which he was able to win over thousands to the Faith wherever he went and to win their passionate devotion. The faith planted by him lasts to today. In 1638, Japan closed its gates to foreigners and tried to uproot the Church and eradicate nearly a century of Jesuit progress. In the purge, 40,000 Christians were martyred by beheading or crucifixion rather than deny their faith, probably the largest group of martyrs in the history of the Church. Of the 100 Jesuit martyrs listed, 44 were Japanese. Xavier was declared the Patron of Navigators as well as, along with St. Theresa of Lisieux, the Patron Saint of all Missions. (Ban, Cor, Ham, JLx, O'M, Som, Tyl)

John Young
(Irish: 1589-1664)

John Young

John was the Novice Director at Kilkenny and Tertian Director in Cork. His frankness and dedication impressed Mercure Verdier, the official Visitor to Ireland sent by the General Carafa to find ways to help the beleaguered Irish Jesuits. The Visitor was impressed by the Irish Jesuits' ability to work hard and endure poverty but he was taken aback by their offering public prayers for a pirate who had helped the Jesuits out in time of financial need. The visitation occurred just before the annihilation of the Irish Mission which was brought to an abrupt halt by the 12,000 seasoned soldiers of Oliver Cromwell in 1649. John was then summoned to become the director of the Irish College in Rome. At his death the General directed that his portrait be painted and his eulogy be preached in the refectory of the Roman College. (Ham, McR)

Nicolas   Zucchi
(Italian: 1586-1670)

Nicolas   Zucchi

Nicolas taught mathematics at the Roman College. Laland speaks with great admiration of his work in perfecting the reflecting telescope. He designed an apparatus which uses a lens to observe the image focused from a concave mirror. This was the model for many of the later designs by scientists such as Isaac Newton. He lived in a time of scientists who held both ingenious ideas together with extravagant errors. For instance he taught that the sun was further from the earth in summer, evident from the need to alter the telescope length; but he also held that Venus was further from earth than Mercury. Nicolas was held in such great esteem that he was sent as a papal legate to the court of the Hapsburg Emperor Ferdinand II of Austria. There he met Kepler, which Nicolas considered one of the most important events of his life. (DSB, Ham, JLx, Som)

An extra glimpse of the early Society

One of the most touching of Kepler's letters was the dedication of his last book, *The Dream by Johannes Kepler* (1634) which contains a long letter of gratitude to Jesuit Paul Guldin who had asked Nicolas Zucchi, a well-known telescope maker, to bring Kepler a telescope. In part it reads:

"To the very reverend Father Paul Guldin, priest of the Society of Jesus, venerable and learned man, beloved patron. There is hardly anyone at this time with whom I would rather discuss matters of astronomy than with you. Even more of a pleasure to me, therefore, was the greeting from your reverence which was delivered to me by members of your order who are here. Fr. Zucchi could not have entrusted this most remarkable gift - I speak of the telescope - to anyone whose effort in this connection pleases me more than yours. I think you should receive from me the first literary fruit of the joy that I gained from trial of this gift [the telescope].

Bibliography

Ashworth, William B. *Jesuit science in the age of Galileo.*
    Kansas City: Lowell Press, 1986
Bangert, William, S.J. *A History of the Society of Jesus.*
Basset, Bernard, S.J. *The English Jesuits.* New York: Herder & Herder, 1968
Brodrick, James, S.J. *The Progress of the Jesuits.* New York: Longmans, 1947
Campbell, Thomas, S.J. *The Jesuits.* London: 1921
Corley, Francis, S.J. *Wings of Eagles.* Chicago: Loyola, 1965
Durant, Will and Ariel *The Story of Civilization.*
    New York: Simon & Schuster, 1963
Encyclopedia Britannica. 24 Vols. Chicago: Benton, 1959
Fülöp-Miller, René *The Power and the Secret of the Jesuits.*
    New York: Viking, 1930
Gerard, John, S.J. *The Autobiography of a Hunted Priest.*
    Chicago: Thomas More, 1952
Gillispie, Charles. C. Ed., *Dictionary of Scientific Biography.* 16 volumes.
    New York: Charles Scribner and Sons, 1970
Grand Dictionnaire Universel 17 vols. Larousse, Pierre,
    Paris: Grand Dictionaire-Universel
Hamy, Alfred, S.J. *Galerie illustree.* Paris: chez l'auteur, 1893-96
Harney, Martin, S.J. *The Jesuits in History.* New York: America, 1941
Hollis, Christopher *The Jesuits: A History.* New York: Macmillan,1968
Jesuit Yearbook. Rome: Curia Generalizia S.J.,1960-1997
Koch, Ludwig, S.J. *Jesuiten Lexicon.* Löwen: Verlag der Bibliothek S.J.,1962
Lacouture, Jean *Jesuits a Multibiography.*
    ˙Washington: Counterpoint, 1995
Linberg, David & Numbers, Ronald (Ed.) *God and Nature.*
    Berkeley: UCB Press, 1986
McDonough, Peter *Men Astutely Trained.* New York: Free Press, 1992
McNaspy, S.J., C.J. and Blanch, J.M.*Lost Cities of Paraguay.*
    Chicago: Loyola, 1982
McRedmond, Louis *To the Greater Glory.* New York: MacMillan, 1991
Mitchell, David *The Jesuits a History.* New York: Franklin Watts, 1981
Mertz, James, S.J. and Murphy, John, S.J. *Jesuit Latin Poets.*
    Wauconda: Bolchazy-Carducci, 1989
Molinari, Paul, S.J. (Ed.) *Companions of Jesus.*
    London: English Province, S.J.,1974
O'Malley, John, S.J. *The First Jesuits.* Cambridge: Harvard, 1993
Philosophical Transactions of the Royal Society. Vols. 1-30.
    London: 1665-1715
Sommervogel, Carolus *Bibliothèque de la compagnie de Jésus.* 12 volumes.
    Bruxelles: Société Belge de Libraire, 1890-1960
Southy, Robert *History of Brazil.* New York: Greenwood, 1969
Tanner, Mathia, S.J. *Societas Jesu.*
    Prague: Universitatis Carolo-Ferdinandae, 1675
Tylenda, Joseph, S.J. *Jesuit Saints and Martyrs.* Chicago: Loyola, 1984
Woodstock Letters. 98 Vols. Woodstock College: Woodstock, MD, 1872-1969

At the end of each sketch the eleven triliteral symbols

(Ban, Bas, DSB, Ham, JLx, McR, JLP, O'M, Som, Tan, Tyl)

signify that the information for the sketches came from the following eleven books which are documented in the bibliography above.

Ban	=	Bangert, William, S.J. *A History of the Society of Jesus*
Bas	=	Basset, Bernard, S.J. *The English Jesuits*
DSB	=	Gillispie, Charles. C. Ed., *Dictionary of Scientific Biography*
Ham	=	Hamy, Alfred, S.J. *Galerie illustree*
JLx	=	Koch, Ludwig, S.J. *Jesuiten Lexicon*
McR	=	McRedmond, Louis *To the Greater Glory.*
JLP	=	Mertz, James, S.J. and Murphy, John, S.J. *Jesuit Latin Poets*
O'M	=	O'Malley, John, S.J. *The First Jesuits*
Som	=	Sommervogel, Carolus *Bibliothèque de la compagnie de Jésus*
Tan	=	Tanner, Mathia, S.J. *Societas Jesu.*
Tyl		= Tylenda, Joseph, S.J. *Jesuit Saints and Martyrs*

Appendices

Appendix I   Jesuit Lunar Craters

Num	Name	Nationality	born-died
1	Mario Bettini	(Italian)	1582-1657
2	Jacques de Billy	(French)	1602-1679
3	Giuseppe Biancani	(Italian)	1566-1624
4	Roger J Boscovich	(Croatian)	1711-1787
5	Nicolas Cabei	(Italian)	1586-1650
6	Christopher Clavius	(German)	1538-1612
7	Jean-Baptiste Cysat	(Swiss)	1588-1657
8	François de Vico	(French)	1805-1848
9	Gyula Fényi	(Hungarian)	1845-1927
10	George Fournier	(French)	1595-1652
11	Francesco Grimaldi	(Italian)	1613-1663
12	Chris. Grienerger	(Swiss)	1564-1636
13	Johann Hagen	(Austrian)	1847-1930
14	Maximilian Hell	(Hungarian)	1720-1792
15	Athanasius Kircher	(German)	1602-1680
16	Francis X Kugler	(German)	1862-1929
17	Charles Malapert	(French)	1580-1630
18	Christian Mayer	(German)	1719-1783
19	Paul McNally	(American)	1890-
20	Theodore Moretus	(Belgian)	1601-1667
21	Denis Petau	(French)	1583-1652
22	Jean-Bap. Riccioli	(Italian)	1598 -1671
23	Matteo Ricci	(Italian)	1552-1610
24	Rodés	(Hungarian)	1881-1939
25	Romaña	(Spanish)	?
26	Christophe Scheiner	(German)	1575-1650
27	George Schömerger	(German)	1597-1645
28	Ange Secchi	(Italian)	1818-1878
29	Hughues Semple	(Scottish)	1596-1654
30	Gerolamo Sirsalis	(Italian)	1584-1654
31	Johan Stein	(Dutch)	1871-1951
32	André Tacquet	(Belgian)	1612-1660
33	Adam Tannerus	(Austrian)	1572-1632
34	Nicolas Zucchi	(Italian)	1586-1670
35	Jean-Baptiste Zupi	(Italian)	1590-1650

Past selenographs listed 5 other Jesuit craters no longer on the NASM list.

Num	Name	Nationality	born-died
36	Andre Arzet	(French)	1604-1675
37	Daniello Bartoli	(Italian)	1608-1685
38	Jean Derienes	(French)	1591-1662
39	Rivas		?
40	Tibor		?

Appendix I
Lunar craters named to honor Jesuits

On page 212 is found a list of the craters named to honor Jesuit scientists and is taken from the National Air and Space Museum (**NASM**) catalog. Recently the International Astronomical Union (**IAU**), founded in 1922, codified lunar nomenclature eliminating conflicts: 35 are named after Jesuits. For centuries the basic map used for lunar nomenclature was the first complete selenograph drawn in 1645 by the Jesuit astronomer, Francesco Grimaldi and published by John Baptist Riccioli, S.J. Today this map is found at the lunar exhibit at the Smithsonian Institute in Washington, D.C.

Grimaldi's 1651 selenograph at the Smithsonian

Numbers mark the locations of 35 lunar craters named after Jesuits. Some of the craters (indicated by arrows) are on the far side of the moon.   The rest can be located by using as a reference the triangle K C T which identifies the three large craters; Kepler, Copernicus and Tycho all of which have distinctive "crater streaks" radiating from them somewhat like the stem of an orange.

Appendix II Jesuit Astronomy and Aeronautics in commemorative stamps

Here are shown 18 of the many commemorative stamps honoring the Jesuit contributions to Astronomy and Aeronautics.

1-4. The Jesuit Astronomical Observatory in Rome These four Vatican stamps honor the *Specola Vaticana* at the Papal Palace in Castelgandolfo. Under Jesuit direction since 1582 it is the oldest observatory in the Western World. Today, observations, are also carried out in Tucson, AR.

5. The Jesuit Astronomical Observatory in Manila A 1971 Philippine stamp celebrates 400 years of Jesuit Astronomical Observations.

6. Matteo Ricci, S.J. (1552-1610) A 1983 Chinese stamp celebrates this Italian Jesuit whose knowledge of mathematics made him the court mathematician in Peking where he introduced trigonometric instruments, translated Euclid and published the first maps of China ever seen by the West.

7. Maximilian Hell, S.J. (1720 - 1792) A 1970 Czechoslovakian stamp honors this Hungarian astronomer, dressed as a Laplander. It was there that he was first to observe a transit of Venus. He was director of the astronomy observatory in Vienna. A lunar crater is named after him.

8. Roger Boscovich, S.J. (1711-1787) A 1987 Yugoslavian stamp honors this Croatian Jesuit astronomer showing the observatory in Milan which Boscovich designed. "Yugoslavia's greatest genius" tracked solar eclipses, perfected the ring micrometer and the achromatic telescope. A lunar crater is named after him. After his death his works were dispersed throughout the world in libraries such as the special Boscovich Archives at Berkeley.

9. Christopher Clavius, S.J. (1538-1612) A 1982 Vatican stamp shows the German Jesuit who was one to whom scholars and potentates would entrust the most sensitive scientific problems of his day. His ubiquitous geometry book led to his being called the *Euclid of the 16th Century.*

10-12. Angelo Pietro Secchi, S.J. (1818-1878) A 1979 series of Vatican stamps honors this Italian Jesuit astronomer. The three instruments perfected by Secchi are shown in the stamps: the meteorograph, the spectroscope and the telescope. Astronomers call him "the Father of Astrophysics".

13. José de Acosta, S.J. (1540-1600) A 1965 Spanish stamp honors this Spanish Jesuit who has been called the *Pliny of the New World.* For his work on altitude sickness in the Andes he is considered a pioneer of modern aeronautical medicine: "He opened the way for aeronautical medical research".

14-16. Francesco Lana Terzi, S.J. (1631 - 1687) Belize, Mali and Zaire stamps honor this Italian physicist. The distinctive four metallic balloons are found in the literature on the history of flight. Lana's 1670 work predates by a century the first balloon flight. He is called the "Father of Aeronautics."

17-18. Bartolomeu Lourenço de Gusmao, S.J. (1685-1724) Two 1985 and 1987 Brazilian stamps honors this Brazilian Jesuit physicist/inventor and commemorates his public 1709 demonstration at the royal court in Lisbon, in the presence of King John III.

Some Jesuit Commemorative Stamps
concerning Astronomy and Aeronautics

Astronomy and Aeronautics

Astronomy

1   2   3
Centenary of the Jesuit Specola Vaticana (Today in Tucson, AR. as well as Rome)

4 Vatican   5 Manila

6 Ricci   7 Hell   8 Boscovich   9 Clavius

Secchi's 1851 meteorograph 10   spectroscope 11   telescope 12   aeronautical medicine of
13 José de Acosta

Aeronautica

14   16   18
Lana Terzi's 1670 airship   Gusmao's 1709 balloon

15   17

Appendix III   Andrea Pozzo's triumphant   ceiling   in the St. Ignatius Church in Rome

One of the most remarkable sights in Rome is the perspective painting on the ceiling of St. Ignatius Church done by the Jesuit brother Andrea Pozzo, a geometer-artist. On the flat, massive ceiling of the church he painted a fresco, in perspective, of the missionary spirit of Jesuit Society, thereby expressing Jesuit identification with the baroque spirit of Rome. Ignatius sends his men to the four corners of the globe. Another Jesuit, Orazio Grassi, S.J. (d 1654), was the architect for the church, but it was Andrea who started a new trend in decorating Jesuit churches.

Several books have been written about Pozzo's contributions to *Jesuit iconography,* but he is best remembered as one of the most influential perspective theorists of the 17th century. Andrea wrote a remarkable book on perspective geometry for artists and architects, *Prospettiva de' pittori ed architetti* (Rome, 1693-1700). This book on perspective transformations in two volumes, has been reprinted many times and, originally written in Latin and Italian, has been translated into French, German, English, Dutch and Chinese. It has been reissued as recently as 1971. In it he demonstrated how an irregular space could be represented on a stage by using wings obliquely. He emphasized the theoretical possibilities of perspective geometry concerning one focal point (for example, the circle of red marble on the floor of St. Ignatius Church is the proper focal point for viewing the ceiling). Andrea Pozzo expressed a new tendency in freer use of decorative elements in stage design. He tried to find a focal point of the perspective out of sight of the audience by displacing it to one side, thereby creating a more realistic effect. Three centuries later the cinema would put into practice some of his principles.

Andrea Pozzo's magnificant soaring allegory of Jesuit missionary work on the ceiling of th St.Ignatius Church in Rome

Appendix IV Clavius Mathematics Group
at the Institut des Hautes Études Scientifiques
in France during July 1992

Clavius Mathematics Group boasts of 27 mathematicians who spend six weeks each summer working together in mathematical research. For the past 34 years they have been meeting on college campuses such as Georgetown, Loyola, McGill, Notre Dame, Berkeley, Holy Cross, Boston College, Princeton and Fairfield as well as twelve summers at three research institutes; The Institute for Advanced Studies in Princeton, New Jersey, the *Centro de Investigacion del Instituto Politecnico Nacional* in Mexico, and the Institut des Hautes Études Scientifiques in Bures-sur-Yvette in France. The purpose of having the meetings in a university setting is to interact with the members of the host mathematics department. Twelve of the members of the Clavius Group are religious. The remaining 15 lay mathematicians attend with their families so that the total number comes to about 40 individuals during a given summer session. This number is never constant, however, since other participating colleagues attend for shorter periods of time. Although most members are from the United States, nine other countries are represented: Italy, France, Brazil, Colombia, Canada, Spain, Dominican Republic, Poland and Germany. All the mathematicians in the group teach in some college or university.

Clavius Mathematics Group in July 1992
Institut des Hautes Études Scientifiques

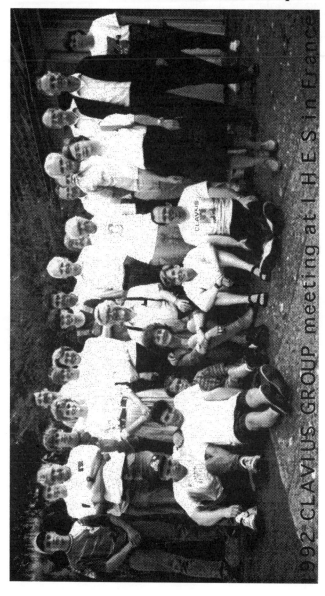

This book, JESUIT FAMILY ALBUM, concerns 202 Jesuit scholars, scientists, artists, explorers and saints who impacted history during the first two and a half centuries of Jesuit history. One of the most famous scholar was Christopher Clavius shown here presenting his reformed calendar to Pope Gregory XIII. Christopher urged the formation of a group to provide mutual support and inspiration for mathematicians to keep abreast of the latest mathematical developments. *"Let an academy be formed for the advancement of mathematics"* In 1963 such a group was formed, The Clavius Group. The proceeds made from contributions for this book will be put into the *Clavius Endowment Fund* (**CLEF**) for the support of the Clavius Group of research mathematicians which carries out the mandate of Christopher Clavius. (The root of Clavius' name, *'key'*, is rendered *CLEF* in French).

Clavius' calendar on the monument to Pope Gregory XIII: St. Peter's Basilica, Vatican City